PHOENIX
BEER

PHOENIX BEER

A History Rising to New Peaks

DAVE CLARK

AMERICAN PALATE

Published by American Palate
A Division of The History Press
Charleston, SC
www.historypress.com

Front cover: Aerial view of downtown Phoenix, Arizona. *Library of Congress Prints and Photographs Division*.

Images from the author's collection unless otherwise noted.

First published 2019

Manufactured in the United States

ISBN 9781467140980

Library of Congress Control Number: 2019948156

Notice: The information in this book is true and complete to the best of our knowledge. It is offered without guarantee on the part of the author or The History Press. The author and The History Press disclaim all liability in connection with the use of this book.

This book is dedicated to my mom for instilling me with a firm grip of the English language early on,

To my wife, Serena, for her encouragement, and

To my daughter Arianne for exemplifying how to chase your dreams

CONTENTS

Preface   9
Acknowledgements   15
Introduction   19

1. Pre-Prohibition Brewing   23
2. Arizona Brewing Company   28
3. Dawning of the Golden Age of Brewing in Phoenix   41
4. The Rise of Four Peaks Brewing Company   53
5. The Modern Era of Brewing in Phoenix   64
   Central Phoenix Breweries   64
   East Valley Breweries   92
   West Valley Breweries   160

About the Author   175

PREFACE

What qualifies one single person to write a book about an entire city's beer history? The answer lies in equal parts desire, knowledge and passion.

There may be beer enthusiasts who have spent their entire lives in Phoenix, engrained in the fabric of the local beer scene longer than I have been. Some may have more established track records as authors. At the end of the day, writing about beer is an expression of passion. For this author, beer is both a passion and a journey.

While my time spent as a resident Arizonan has been relatively brief, my love for beer dates back to a time before I was legally allowed to consume the beverage. Commencing with a beer can collection as a pre-teenager leading to an eventual career as a professional brewer and Master level beer judge, I've come full circle with beer and have been involved with it intricately over the years in many different capacities.

As with many teenagers, beer, at first, was a party starter. It didn't take long, however, for me to be able to determine a good beer from a bad one, and I honed my palate relatively quickly. Even as a teenager with very little disposable income, I got resourceful finding the extra few dollars needed to purchase premium beers over cheaper alternatives. With a preference for Canadian lagers, I was a beer snob-in-training before I even knew it.

As rock band members with a weekend off, a bandmate and I were planning to spend the day at Kings Island amusement park near Cincinnati, Ohio, for a day of roller coaster adventures. The plans changed suddenly when the skies opened and sheets of water cascaded down.

With time to burn, Waffle House was on our radar following a late night of enjoying the aforementioned Canadian lagers at a nearby rock club. Traveling north on I-75 just south of the Ohio River, we saw a sign that beckoned us, announcing "brewery tour this exit." We postponed our search for grease and caffeine in exchange for a little "hair of the dog." Youthful indiscretions.

As we approached the red brick fortress that was Oldenberg Brewery of Fort Mitchell, Kentucky, excitement began to build. We took the forty-five-minute brewery tour, which promised free samples upon its conclusion.

The tour took us from a room filled with one of the world's largest breweriana collections through the brewhouse, where we witnessed the sights, sounds and smells of fresh beer being made. The wonderful aromatics of the marriage of malt and hops captivated me, forever changing the neural pathways of my brain. I needed to learn and experience more about beer.

When the tour concluded, we gathered in the tasting room to enjoy our five, five-ounce samples of Oldenberg's beers. One after another was a sensory extravaganza. I was used to beer tasting like, well, beer, but this was a whole new world. A beer connoisseur was born.

On that given day, I recall Oldenberg featuring a wheat beer, a light blonde, a raspberry ale, a pale ale and the showstopper, their signature Vienna-style lager called OPV (Oldenberg Premium Verum). Although I didn't know one style from the next, I knew I loved everything about the entire experience. These twenty-five ounces of one brewery's beer opened my eyes to the potential of what beer had to offer. A new advocate for what would later be called the craft beer movement was born at that brewery.

Always wanting to be the first kid on the block with a new toy, I bought as many cases as my wallet (and trunk space) would allow and brought this newfound beer back home to share with my close circle of friends. If nothing more, the quality of the beer at band practice would take an immediate turn for the better.

A few years later, *microbrew* started to be called *craft beer*. That subtle change seemed to invite a new generation of beer consumers eager to discover an alternative to the mass-produced, uninspired lagers from mega-breweries of the day.

The more I learned and the more I experienced, the more I got into it. I brewed my own batch of beer at a local brew-your-own facility in the early 2000s. That led to learning how to brew at home, first on the stove, then upgrading to a full mini-brewery in the garage.

I bought the required texts for beer knowledge, such as Dave Miller's *Homebrewing Guide* and John Palmer's *How to Brew*. I joined the American Homebrewers Association, and I subscribed to *Brew Your Own Magazine*. I joined the local Cleveland homebrew club called S.N.O.B., of which I became president just a few years later. I made it a point to get to know every local brewer on a first-name basis—a fairly easy achievement considering the amount of time I spent at their various establishments.

My interest in brewing became an obsession. While many fellow amateurs were happy brewing a batch now and then, I'd spend all day brewing double batches, at times having as many as eleven different styles available at once. This required the manufacture of a kegerator, which turned out to be a six-tap work of art, designed by good friend Brian Kelly. (Thanks, Brian.)

I entered competitions regularly and started winning medals. I got involved with an organization known as the Beer Judge Certification Program (BJCP), which is, essentially, a group of like-minded individuals that drink beer, discuss its merits and grade it accordingly. This really exists, and I was more than happy to participate.

Quickly, I worked my way up the ranks of the BJCP, eventually achieving the Master level. Reaching Master is a level that only about 2 percent of judges reach. At the time of this writing, I'm proud to say that I am one of only two Master-level judges in the state of Arizona.

Fulfilling a dream, I got an opportunity to become a brewer at an Akron, Ohio brewery called Hoppin' Frog. From that first "brew-your-own" experience, I had now become a professional brewer in the span of about three years. Hard work and determination paid off.

I worked as a professional brewer for the next year and a half and learned a lot. It planted the seed in my mind about opening my own brewery, which I began planning in earnest. Though it never did open, my beer journey continued. Eventually, we moved away from the snow and cold of Cleveland to the dry desert heat of Phoenix, Arizona.

Prior to the Arizona move, I got involved with a fairly new organization called Cicerone, marketed as the beer industry's answer to wine's sommelier program. Passing the Cicerone exam on the first try, scoring a very respectable 87, I now had pretty good credentials as a former professional brewer, a highly ranked BJCP judge and a Certified Cicerone. It was nice to have validated recognition of the knowledge I had acquired after countless hours of study and hands-on application.

After becoming established in Arizona, I became the local beer writer for both the *New Times* and *Entertainer Magazine* and began writing for national

beer magazines, including *Brew Your Own Magazine*. This gave me the amazing opportunity to contribute to the very magazine from which I learned how to brew when I started my beer journey.

Life is about living your passions, and I live my two passions, craft beer and music, with regularity. Today, I perform regularly throughout the metro Phoenix area as a singer/guitarist and have released a full-length album of original material titled *Rock City*. The album is named after the brewery concept that I never opened. You never know how your inspiration is going to manifest itself; you just have to be open to the possibilities.

Must-Try Beers of Phoenix

Every effort has been made in this book to tell the stories about the people behind Phoenix's breweries without interjecting any personal bias or opinion. This section is the sole exception. If you want to experience the absolute best the city's brewing scene has to offer, these are the five beers you want to enjoy. Let the disagreements begin!

5. Grooving With The Pict, North Mountain. 6.3% ABV, 21 IBU. This may not be the most popular Scottish ale in Phoenix, but it is the tastiest and most true to style. Rich malt with just a hint of smoke leads to a clean finish.

4. Hatch Chile Gatos, Fate. 4.8% ABV, 23 IBU. This cream ale features the addition of hatch chiles that provide a welcoming clean pepper flavor with very little heat. A true taste of the Southwest. Fate Irish Red and Mexican (Vienna) Lager receive honorable mention.

3. Valley Venom Pilsner, Helton. 4.9% ABV, 12 IBU. In a world of barrel-aged, double imperial sour beers with fruit, sometimes simple prevails. This one-malt, one-hop work of art showcases the brewing talents of Brian Helton with a beer perfectly crafted for the Phoenix climate. Maybe a helles, maybe a pilsner, but unquestionably delicious.

2. White Russian, Sun Up. 9.4% ABV, 65 IBU. Flavors and aromas of coffee, bittersweet chocolate, caramel, vanilla, raisin and plum intersect to create a symphony of palate destruction, in a good way. Full bodied and creamy, this is a great sipping beer.

1. Bière Blanche, Pedal Haus. 5.1% ABV, 14 IBU. A traditional witbier crafted with Moroccan orange peel and coriander. A true Belgian masterpiece brewed in the heart of Sun Devil country by the legendary Derek Osborne.

ACKNOWLEDGEMENTS

This book is dedicated to everyone who has played a role in furthering my knowledge and appreciation of all things beer. To Frank Barickman, Paul Shick and Nelson Crowle for sharing their vast brewing knowledge, helping me to achieve my goal of becoming a Master BJCP judge; to Fred Karm for mentoring me during my time brewing professionally at Hoppin' Frog Brewery; and to Nick Pauley for giving me the honor of being your mentor—you've done great, kid!

To Mike Habrat for continuously raising the bar when it comes to brewing and beer knowledge.

Left: *Phoenix Beer* author Dave Clark (*left*) and former Arizona Wilderness brewer Nicholas Pauley.

Right: Dave Clark and Mike Habrat. From high school classmates to Master BJCP beer judges.

To every single professional brewer friend who has taken time away from their unforgiving schedules to answer my questions or help me complete a feature story, especially Fat Heads' Matt Cole, New Realm's Mitch Steele and Market Garden's Andy Tveekrem.

To all the Phoenix brewers and brewery owners who dedicated their time in order for me to properly capture their stories.

To my editor, Lindsey Givens, who was a true pleasure to work with, and to all at Arcadia Publishing for making this book possible.

I thank every single person who participated in making this book become a reality. Every beer I enjoyed was as great as the conversations the beers accompanied. Getting to know the people who make up the fabric of the Phoenix beer scene was both rewarding and memorable. Most of all, I want to personally thank each and every person who bought this book. Thanks for reading and for wanting to learn a little more about what makes Phoenix beer special. Cheers!

SOURCES

A good part of the book, especially the modern-era information, stems from live interviews from key people in and around the Phoenix beer scene, usually brewery owners and brewers. Other resources were also used, such as online articles, websites and expertise of individuals.

The main source for the historical aspect of the book (chapters 1–3) is *Brewing Arizona*, written by Ed Sipos, a detailed text about the history of Arizona brewing. While *Phoenix Beer* specifically focuses on breweries in and around Phoenix, Ed's book provides a historical perspective of beer and breweries statewide and is a must-read for anyone who enjoys beer, history or a little of both. His extensive collection of vintage photos alone is worth the book's purchase price.

Ed is the foremost expert on the history of Arizona beer, and I feel no need to try to compete with his esteemed work. Ed was gracious enough to talk with me at length, share his vast collection of vintage beer memorabilia for photos and allow me to often reference his text for historical information. Rather than filling the pages of *Phoenix Beer*

Phoenix Beer author Dave Clark and *Brewing Arizona* author Ed Sipos.

with endless footnotes, rest assured that *Brewing Arizona* was the primary source for the majority of the historical information contained herein. I am very thankful for Ed's willingness to help and share his knowledge. A fine author and even a finer man, Mr. Sipos is a true class act.

INTRODUCTION

History of Beer in Phoenix

The challenges the earliest brewers of the hot Phoenix valley faced are brought to light in this book, as are the devastating effects Prohibition delivered to the beer industry. Influential breweries that created the historical fabric of the Phoenix beer scene are illustrated, especially the once proud Arizona Brewing Company that was an Arizona brewing icon for decades.

This book provides a lengthy history of Phoenix beer but focuses more so on the here and now. Understanding the history gives us perspective on how the Phoenix brewing scene evolved into what it has become today, but reading stories about breweries where you can go and have a beer today has its advantages. That was the impetus behind making the book skew more toward the modern-day brewing scene that continues to grow, develop and mature.

How to Use This Book

This book is a collection of stories of everyday people who had a vision and saw their vision come to life. While there is a chronological flow of the book's first four chapters, the breweries of the modern-day section are presented alphabetically and geographically, making it easier for readers to locate specific breweries.

UNDERSTANDING BEER TERMINOLOGY

It would be helpful to understand a few key terms in order for the book to make sense. ABV refers to a beer's alcohol by volume, a measure of how much alcohol a particular beer has relative to the volume of the beer itself. A 5% ABV beer, therefore, has 5 percent alcohol, by volume, and 95 percent everything else (mostly water).

IBU refers to International Bitterness Units, a measure of bitterness found in beer, specifically derived from hops. There is a distinct difference between "hoppy" and "bitter." Bitterness refers to the dry sensation in the back of the palate upon swallowing a beer, which comes from extracting bittering compounds from hops during the boiling process. "Hoppiness" refers to the hop flavor and aroma compounds found in a hop-forward beer, derived from the oils of a hop cone. A beer can be very hoppy yet not bitter, while a hoppy beer can also be extremely bitter. A non-hoppy beer can be bitter, as well. It's all reflected in the art of the brewmaster.

A lesser used term in the book, SRM, measures a beer's color. SRM stands for Standard Reference Method and produces a scale ranging from 0 to 40+. The larger the number, the darker the beer. For reference, a light-colored beer such as Coors Light (straw to yellow in color) will have an SRM near 2, while a dark stout such as Guinness will have an SRM beyond 40. Any beer with an SRM over 40 will be black. An IPA often checks in around 7–10 SRM.

A QUICK NOTE ON BEER STYLES

All beers are made to represent a specific style, or type, of beer. Creating styles gives beer drinkers a general understanding of what to expect from their beer. While certainly there is differentiation within a style, it is well established that a porter or stout beer will be dark in color and have roasted, chocolate-like notes and a fairly thick body. Styles help us understand and appreciate beer and the differences between beers.

When it comes to putting beer styles in writing, a natural quandary exists. Some styles represent cities of origin, such as Pilsner (which originates from Pilsen, Czech Republic), and some even represent the month the beer was traditionally made, such as Marzen, the German word for March. Cities and months are traditionally capitalized, but seeing a list of styles with some capitalized and others not makes for a strange read. Therefore, accept the fact that for consistency, the styles will be presented in this book in all lower case.

How This Book Came to Be

One of the biggest challenges in writing this book is trying to cover as many breweries as possible and tell their stories fully, without ending up with the next *War and Peace* or exceeding the publisher's word count limit. This book tells the stories about the people behind the breweries, more so than focusing on the beer itself. Since it's intended to be a light, easy read, I elected to cover many of the area's breweries, but not all, telling those stories as thoroughly as possible.

The decision on which to cover or not cover came organically. Attempts were made to connect with as many breweries as possible. The goal was to conduct as many live, in-person interviews as possible and settle for phone calls as a backup. In some cases, email conversations and website references sufficed.

In situations where no direct contact could be made, resulting in a lack of information, the decision was made to exclude those breweries from the book. In no way does inclusion or exclusion, or length of the individual stories, imply any sort of preference or ranking of the local breweries or any personal bias whatsoever.

1
PRE-PROHIBITION BREWING

In today's instant gratification world, we often take for granted how easy it is to find beer. Visit your local watering hole, restaurant or grocery store, and options abound. For those adventurous souls who prefer to create their own, a trip to the local homebrew store for barley, hops and yeast ensures that beer can be made in the confines of one's home. It was not always so easy, and especially not in the extreme heat of the Phoenix valley.

In the mid-1800s, when the first semblances of breweries began to appear, making beer was challenging. The desert heat made growing barley and hops, the heart and soul of beer, difficult, if not impossible. Yeast, the magical organism that turns sugar water into beer, was just being discovered and not fully understood. The lifeblood of beer—water—required a clean source containing the proper balance of pH and minerals essential for brewing, something that the valley's brackish water lacked.

Interstate commerce was just being developed and was not yet a viable option for importing the needed supplies. Since pasteurization did not yet exist, the need for refrigeration was essential, both for production purposes and storage of the beer.

If these challenges weren't enough to deter even the most dedicated, imagine early brewers standing over a boiling kettle for hours in a non-air-conditioned facility where external temperatures regularly exceed 115 degrees. One can truly appreciate the challenges that faced the earliest brewers of the Phoenix valley.

Breweries of the day existed to serve the neighborhood, rather than distributing far and wide as they do today. The few breweries that managed to open for business often did not last long. Until recently, only one brewery, the Arizona Brewing Company, enjoyed consistent success in the Phoenix market, and even it faced a fair share of challenges and obstacles. But it all had to start somewhere, and Phoenix's brewing roots trace back to a brewery that shared the city's name, the Phoenix Brewery.

PHOENIX BREWERY: THE FIRST BREWERY OF PHOENIX

The first brewery in Phoenix owes its roots to the small northwestern town of Wickenburg, about sixty minutes northwest of the big city. It was here that Abraham Peeples ran the Magnolia Saloon and Brewery, where he was both the proprietor and brewer. A man with many interests, Peeples wanted to expand his operation into the growing, newly named city to the southeast called Phoenix. He and an associate purchased plots of land and opened a brewery named after the city.

Peeples built the Phoenix Brewery in 1871 in the area that is now considered to be 1st and 2nd Streets, near Washington Street. His many interests in Wickenburg led him to sell to the new brewery rather quickly to his friend and brother-in-law, Mathew Cavaness. Cavaness ran the business with a man he brought in to be his business partner, a blacksmith named Frank Cosgrove. Cavaness brewed the company's beer once a week. The two ran the brewery until April 1873, when they sold it back to Peeples, who then brought in Thomas Hayes to be a partner in the brewery.

Just two months later, Peeples again sold his portion of the brewery, and the brewery took on a new name of Hayes & Lovejoy's Brewery and Saloon. Half a decade later, in 1878, the brewery once again had a new owner, former Tucson resident Albert Sales. He renamed the brewery Champion Brewery. Operating through the mid-1880s, Champion Brewery was reportedly taken out by a fire that destroyed an entire block of businesses.

The Arcade Brewery

In 1879, the former mayor of Prescott, Charles August Luke, moved to Phoenix and created the Arcade Brewery. Along with partner Joseph Thalheimer, this small brewery was constructed of red brick, something new for the Phoenix area, where adobe construction was the norm. Despite its size, Arcade enjoyed a steady following, which kept the partners brewing almost daily.

In 1884, Michael Wurch bought Thalheimer's interest in the business. Formerly of the St. Louis Brewing and Malting Company, the company advertised its beer as being "the finest beer ever made in the territory and equal in every way to the St. Louis imported beer." Wurch remained at the brewery for the next three years, working alongside his two sons. As of 1888, the brewery was no longer, and not much is known of why it ceased to exist.

During this period, much progress was made, especially in the realms of transportation and refrigeration, which meant beer could be imported into Phoenix. With the brackish water of Phoenix, it must have been hard to produce beers that could rival those made in locations with great water sources.

Phoenicians simply wanted good-tasting beer. No efforts were made to promote drinking local, as we often see today, and there was not a lot of urgency for entrepreneurs to establish new breweries in this less-than-ideal, hot brewing climate. Not much happened in the realm of local brewing until the turn of the century. Whatever modest progress was being made in the realm of brewing at that time was immediately extinguished with America's great failed experiment known as Prohibition.

Prohibition

No historical account about beer and brewing is complete without considering the impact prohibition had on beer and the brewing industry. While national Prohibition went into effect on January 16, 1920, through ratification of the Eighteenth Amendment and, ultimately, the passage of the Volstead Act, it was decades in the making.

Nationwide, many women were opposed to alcohol and its effects. However, their voices were somewhat stifled lacking the ability to vote. As the women's suffrage movement progressed, it coincided with a female-led temperance movement meant to bring attention to the perceived perils of alcohol. In 1874, the Woman's Christian Temperance Union (WCTU) was formed to create a national voice.

This coincided with the formation of the Anti-Saloon League in 1895, and all of a sudden, support for states becoming dry began to build. Those opposed to alcohol were organized and driven, while the "wets" didn't originally consider opposition forces to be anything other than a bother. Between the WCTU and the Anti-Saloon League, opinions began to shift, including those in the world of politics. Alcohol was positioned as being "sinful," and lawmakers didn't want to legislate in ways that gave the impression they supported sinful activities. Public and political opinions began to shift rather quickly.

Long before Congress passed the Volstead Act in October 1919, Arizona, along with several other states, had already voted to become dry. The Temperance Federation of Arizona was founded in 1914, just two years into Arizona's statehood. Made up of motivated individuals and high-profile leaders, the group worked quickly to change the hearts and minds of those in America's forty-eighth state. On November 3, 1914, a statewide election was held, and in a close vote, the "dries" defeated the "wets" 25,887 to 22,743, officially making Arizona a dry state, effective January 1, 1915. While Phoenix did not yet have a burgeoning brewery scene at the time, it definitely played a huge role in retarding the future growth of Arizona's brewing scene, since making or selling beverages containing alcohol was now unlawful.

National Prohibition went into effect on January 16, 1920, with the belief it would cure many of the country's problems. What it did do was eliminate jobs for people who worked with and in the industry and eradicated tax revenue the industry previously generated. Moreover, it encouraged people to find alternative methods to alter their minds, such as turning to marijuana and stronger drugs, which were legal at the time. Most importantly, it ushered in a black market for alcohol, which led to a substantial increase in organized crime.

The cost of Prohibition was also felt in the huge number of dollars spent to enforce this law, which pushed the country's prisons to capacity. The number of felons rose by 561 percent during Prohibition. Clearly, Prohibition was a failure.

Sentiment changed once again, and a movement to repeal Prohibition began to take shape. With President Franklin Delano Roosevelt fully behind repeal, and with Congress in agreement, the Cullen-Harrison Act was adopted on March 21, 1933, making the manufacture and sale of 3.2% ABV beer legal (where it was not prohibited by state law.) This new law went into effect on April 7, 1933. Later that year, Prohibition was officially repealed with ratification of the Twenty-First Amendment on December 5, 1933, a date that is still regularly celebrated to this day, especially by those in the brewing industry.

2

ARIZONA BREWING COMPANY

Just a month after the production of "near beer" was deemed legal, the Arizona Brewing Company was established by brothers Martin and Herman Fenster. No relation to the Prescott-based brewery of the same name defunct since Prohibition, the brewery was constructed on East Madison Street in Phoenix. Herman Fenster brought years of brewing experience to the newly founded company, having worked for the Cleveland and Sandusky Brewing Company in Ohio.

The brewmaster was Oskar Scholz, a thirty-year veteran of the brewing industry. Having spent much of his career at the renowned Pilsen Brewery of Czechoslovakia, Scholz understood the importance of using pure water to brew good beer. The first beer produced was sold on October 1, 1933, simply called Arizona Brew. After a naming contest was held to give the beer an official name, the name Sunbru was chosen from over ten thousand responses, a name that would weave itself into the fabric of the Phoenix beer scene for years to come.

NEW OWNERSHIP

Despite being the founders of what would become one of Phoenix's most prolific breweries, not much is known of the Fensters. Not unlike McDonald's lore in which Richard and Maurice McDonald are often forgotten while Ray Kroc receives the accolades, much of the credit for the

Left: Apache Beer bottle, circa 1938.

Below: Apache Beer neon sign—chief of them all.

rise of the Arizona Brewing Companies goes to the owners who followed the Fenster brothers.

In early 1934, the brewery was sold to three partners with extensive backgrounds in business and the brewing industry. E.P. Baker was a leader of San Diego's Aztec Brewing Company, Bailey Russell was a former president of the Arizona Liquor Distributors and Wirt Bowman, Russell's father-in-law, was an accomplished entrepreneur and casino owner.

The partners invested heavily into the brewery, putting over $100,000 into renovations that included a twelve-thousand-square-foot addition, a labeling machine/bottling line, a pasteurizer and expanded fermentation that increased the brewery's capacity fourfold.

One of the biggest changes that took place under the new ownership was the introduction of Apache Beer, a lager, in June 1934. This flagship offering spawned several offshoot brands, including Apache Blue Label, English-Type Ale and Bock Beer. Several additional brands were produced under contract as private label offerings.

The beer was first offered as a draft-only option but quickly became available in bottles, and a few years later, in 1936, it was one of the country's first beers offered in cans.

While ownership was aggressive and continuously looking for ways to innovate and grow the brewery, partner Bailey Russell became ill and the brewery was again put up for sale.

ROBERT THE ELDER

Robert Elder, a former president of a huge California distributor, became the new owner in July 1937. With him, he brought Erhardt William (E.W.) "Pop" Lindner to be the brewery's new brewmaster. Lindner would play a huge role in the company's growth and expansion in the years that followed.

Apache Beer and Elder Brau, two successful products of the Arizona Brewing Company.

Being an astute businessman, Elder employed several tactics to cut wasteful spending and operate the brewery more efficiently. Those changes included innovative marketing campaigns that boosted the company's profits and the elimination of the costly-to-operate canning line.

Pop Lindner instituted a new beer in January 1939 called Elder Brau, an all-malt beer named after the new brewery owner. The new beer, along with changes made at the brewery, proved initially successful, but not long-lasting. Just a few years later, profits began to decline, and Elder filed for bankruptcy, leaving the company.

The War's Impact on the Brewing Industry

During this time, the Second World War was beginning to have an effect on the brewing industry in ways never imagined. The war had been mostly a European struggle until the attack on Pearl Harbor changed that in an instant. All of a sudden, the United States was at war with two main adversaries: Japan and Germany.

Not only were supplies affected—from metals for brewing equipment to grain for brewing—but sentiment toward German Americans also changed overnight. German culture was so interwoven into American brewing that people began to have a change of heart about supporting beers that were brewed or influenced by the country's newest adversary. Beers with obvious German influence, including Elder Brau, were quickly falling out of favor. Arizona Brewing Company knew a change was needed—and fast.

Elder Brau tin, circa 1940.

JOSEPH F. LANSER TO THE RESCUE

With Elder out of the picture, a new buyer named Joseph F. Lanser surfaced; he bid $140,000 for a 51 percent majority stake in the brewery. A former brewery executive from Tacoma, Washington, Lanser was a shrewd businessman who was driven to right the Arizona Brewing Company ship.

Having an extensive background in industries connected to brewing, Lanser understood subtle nuances that would positively affect his brewery. He worked as a grain broker, started a grain exporting company and was a lead investor, and later president, of Tacoma's Columbia Brewery. These experiences served Lanser well, and his presence was immediately felt within the brewery's walls.

Lanser reorganized the company, filing articles of incorporation. That change was nowhere near as eventful as the introduction of a simply named flagship offering called A-1 Pilsner Beer in January 1943.

A-1 PILSNER BEER

Once A-1 was introduced, all other beers in the brewery's lineup were phased out, including the popular Apache Beer. The only beer the brewery continued to make outside A-1 was a private label offering for A.J. Bayless Markets known as Dutch Treat.

The introduction of A-1 came at an interesting time in the history of American brewing. Due to shortages of grain because of the war, many American breweries began to employ adjuncts in their beer as a grain replacement. Adjuncts, most notably rice and/or corn, produced a lighter overall character in the beer, cost less to produce and were generally accepted by the public, especially women. Many breweries that perfected this adjunct-rich style formed a stronghold in the brewing industry during this time, including the rise of Anheuser-Busch, Pabst, Schlitz and Coors.

Arizona Brewing Company chose not to employ adjuncts in its beer, considering these ingredients to be inferior, much in the same spirit craft breweries view these ingredients today.

Lanser's innovative marketing tactics, including utilizing radio, television, print and strategically placed point-of-sale messages, made A-1 Beer top of mind throughout the Southwest, pushing the brewery to near capacity at 55,490 barrels in 1945.

Left: A-1 Beer neon.

Below: A-1 authorized dealer sign.

Lanser didn't let a grain shortage derail his company's growth. When he maxed out his grain allotment, he bought a small Minnesota brewery, including its grain supply, to fill the gaps needed to produce A-1. When the grain was used, he resold the brewery, displaying his ingenuity and business savvy.

The popularity of A-1 necessitated the need for expansion. Arizona Brewing Company expanded onto a plot of land near the existing brewery, with a $2 million expansion plan. The new facility came complete with a brand-new canning line, a bottle shop, a warehouse, offices for workers, a

A-1 Lita Baron poster.

shipping and receiving facility and a brand-new brewhouse. The new facility spared no expense and even included loading platforms and railroad spurs to ensure fresh beer could be widely distributed. The new facility could produce upward of 250,000 barrels per year. Fueled by the expansion, the brewery's sales increased 32 percent from 1948 to 1949, the largest increase of any brewery in the United States during this period.

Arizona Brewing Company looked for opportunities to expand its presence and positive image in the marketplace. Frequently entering competitions produced many awards, enabling the company to legitimately use the phrase "Judged the Finest" as its slogan, having proof to back it up. These efforts led to A-1 becoming the most popular beer in Arizona during the first half of the 1950s.

THE TIMES THEY ARE A CHANGING

American palates continued to be drawn to lighter, adjunct-filled beers, moving away from flavorful all-malt beers like A-1. As consumers began to gravitate toward brewing giants such as Anheuser-Busch and Miller, the smaller breweries began to feel the hit. In 1952, company stockholders saw a reduction in dividends for the first time.

As people began to migrate en masse to the Southwest, it actually had a negative effect on the local brewery. Instead of adapting to the local beer, they pledged allegiance to the beers of their birthplace, namely the Midwest. Despite Arizona Brewing Company having a nice distribution footprint in the country's Southwest, the writing was on the wall for the long-term prospects of the company.

By the early 1960s, the A-1 brand had become commonplace, and the beer held less of a special place in the hearts and palates of consumers. On the advice of the company's advertising agency, a new beer was created to replace A-1. The beer was called Lancers, a lighter version of A-1 that used a rare Yugoslavian hop variety known as Backa. While innovative, it changed the entire flavor profile that fans of the brewery had come to expect.

The end of Arizona Brewing Company was on the horizon. E.W. "Pop" Lindner, who had finally retired in 1961 at age eighty-one, passed away two years later in February 1963. Later that year, Joseph F. Lanser Sr. died of a heart attack in December 1963. In tribute, his son, Joseph Lanser Jr., renamed the beer J.F. Lansers the following summer. A fitting tribute, but the change did nothing to spur additional sales.

J.F. Lanser's lamp.

Without the patriarchs of the company around to ensure a consistent level of quality, things began to change, and not for the better. Lesser ingredients were used, and techniques that produced cheaper beer were employed. The brand identity of A-1 that built over many years no longer existed, and the company was at a crossroads. In 1964, the decision was made to put the brewery up for sale.

ENTER CARLING BREWING COMPANY

On October 8, 1964, the Carling Brewing Company officially purchased Arizona Brewing Company, making it the ninth brewery in the company's portfolio. This also signaled the end of the Lansers being involved with the brewery. The Lindners did remain, with Herb becoming the plant's general manager and Max continuing as brewmaster.

Carling looked to upgrade the brewery and invested over $1 million into its newest plant, including the installation of glass-lined tanks. The additional investment increased the brewery's capacity to 350,000 barrels of beer per year.

Through the years: Lancer's, JF Lanser's Carling A-1, A-1 series.

Carling's flagship beer was known as Black Label and had quite a following in other parts of North America. Banking on similar results, Carling made Black Label the flagship beer of the Phoenix brewery. Meanwhile, the A-1 brand did enjoy a short-lived revival in July 1965 when J.F. Lanser's was replaced by Carling A-1. However, not being the primary focus of the brewery caused A-1 to flounder.

Carling expected fans to flock to its Black Label brand, but that following never materialized. Just two years later, the decision was made to put the Phoenix brewery up for sale.

The National Brewing Company

Based in Baltimore, Maryland, the National Brewing Company offered more than $4 million for the plant and became its new owner on November 29, 1966. National now had a brewery in a major southwestern city to go along with its plants in Baltimore, Miami and Detroit.

National made its money selling Colt 45 malt liquor, a beer that skyrocketed to become the country's most popular malt liquor shortly after its introduction in 1963.

Unlike Carling, National Brewing had the wherewithal to focus on the importance of local in much of its marketing. Part of that strategy included reintroducing A-1 in 1967 with a whole new look and an Arizona-based advertising campaign.

National Brewing was on the forefront of co-mingling sports and beer and was an avid sponsor of several teams in various sports. The brewery even acquired the Baltimore Orioles franchise to diversify its portfolio. Sports-centric marketing helped the company for a time, with popularity of both Colt 45 and A-1 increasing. But as so often happens, circumstances beyond the brewery's control had a major effect on the company and its brands.

Miller Brewing purchased a brand called Lite from a small Chicago brewery named Meister Brau and promoted it voraciously. At this time in American history, many beer drinkers stayed loyal to a "personal" brand of beer, not readily willing to experiment between brands or styles. It was much different than the brewery hopping tendencies of today's drinker.

Lite became the popular choice for many, while other brands began to feel the pinch, including Colt 45 and A-1. In fact, National even rebranded A-1

Four cans of the 007 series.

in 1974 as A-1 Light Pilsner to try to keep up with the growing trend toward lighter beers. It made very little difference, and the once proud premium brand A-1 had devolved into a budget bin brand.

Another trend that occurred during this time and continues to this day was the consolidation of breweries. As breweries such as Anheuser-Busch, Pabst and Miller continued to gain exponential market share, other breweries were forced to merge to compete. In 1975, Carling sold its American division to National for $19 million, creating a new company known as Carling-National Breweries Inc. When the merger occurred, the company became the tenth-largest brewer in the country.

Even at number ten, the company just didn't have the financial clout to compete in the ultracompetitive marketing and advertising realm where most beer loyalists were won over. Profits continued to decline, and the brewery also lost part of its heart and soul when the Lindner brothers retired, first Max in 1976 and then Herb, three years later. More consolidation was on the horizon, and, this time, it was G. Heileman Brewing Company that would attempt to save the fortunes of the once proud Arizona Brewing Company.

G. Heileman Brewing Company

On March 27, 1979, the La Crosse, Wisconsin–based G. Heileman Brewing Company purchased Carling-National for over $35 million, giving the behemoth a whopping thirty-four different brands that generated upward of $655 million in revenue.

This was a truly pivotal time in American brewing history. Consolidation had reduced the number of operating breweries in the United States to a historic low of 101, and the number of independently owned breweries was even lower. Numbers such as these had not been seen since Prohibition all but wiped out the industry in the early part of the century.

By no means did this mean people were drinking less beer. Per capita consumption reached a high point of 23.8 gallons in 1981. The wealth was not equally distributed, however. The top five breweries accounted for 76 percent of beer consumption, and the top ten controlled 94 percent. Anheuser-Busch led the way, controlling 30 percent of the market, while Miller remained hot on its heels with 22.5 percent. G. Heileman and its huge portfolio was the fourth-largest brewer with 7.8 percent of the market, just behind Schlitz at 7.9 percent and slightly ahead of Pabst (7.5 percent) and above Coors (7.3 percent), which at this stage did not yet distribute east of the Mississippi.

In the position G. Heileman found itself, everything revolved around scale. Unfortunately for the Phoenix plant, it couldn't produce the scale needed to remain an active part of the company's lineup, and despite honing operations to be as efficient as possible, a decision was made to close the plant once and for all in late March 1985. The major metropolitan area of Phoenix was now without a brewery to call its own.

The Brief Second Life of A-1 Beer

The Phoenix brewery was demolished in May 1993. It took three months to complete the job. The Phoenix fire department built offices on the former site that remain in use today. Any hope of the brewery being purchased and repurposed were now lost forever.

While the building would no longer produce another drop of beer, it didn't necessarily signal the end to A-1 Beer, after all. A popular Arizona liquor chain known as Beverage House was half owned by Eli Drakulich,

Different eras of A-1.

who had fond memories of drinking A-1 Beer. Drakulich wanted to find a way to revive the brand and sell it as a house brand for his liquor chain. After contacting G. Heileman, a deal was struck, and A-1 became Beverage House's in-store budget brand in 1995. For a time, Drakulich was ecstatic.

When Stroh Brewing acquired G. Heileman in July 1996, it also acquired all its brands, including A-1. Stroh had no interest in continuing to produce this brand. Once again, Drakulich was without his beloved A-1.

The creative Drakulich came up with a plan and formed a corporation called the A-1 Beer Company in October 1996. About a month later, he approached Stroh's about acquiring the A-1 trademark. With no plans to produce the beer, Stroh's agreed and Drakulich finally owned the rights to the brand.

Due to liquor laws prohibiting the same person from owning licenses to produce and distribute beer, Drakulich couldn't produce and sell A-1 as long as he was still affiliated with Beverage House. It wasn't until May 2009 that Beverage House liquor was sold and Drakulich was free to finally pursue selling A-1.

Working with Nimbus Brewing Company of Tucson, an agreement was made where Nimbus would brew and distribute the beer and Drakulich would get a portion of the sales. After many years of being relegated to budget-beer status, A-1 was once again a premium brand, with the first bottles appearing on August 10, 2010. Sadly, Drakulich's celebration was short-lived. He died of cancer the following February. Nimbus continued to produce A-1 for about a year until the brewery filed for bankruptcy. A-1 reached the end of the road.

3

DAWNING OF THE GOLDEN AGE OF BREWING IN PHOENIX

The world is all about supply and demand. With such a dearth of brewing companies to choose from, and many of the beers tasting quite similar, an undercurrent of American beer enthusiasts took it upon themselves to improve this country's state of beer. They lived by a simple principle: if you want it done right, do it yourself.

While beer has been made in homes for centuries, it started to gain popularity in the 1970s and 1980s, especially after President Carter signed a bill making homebrewing legal in the United States in 1978. A few years earlier, slightly ahead of the law making it legal, a group of beer lovers assembled in Los Angeles calling themselves the Maltose Falcons, effectively creating the country's first homebrew club.

Information, knowledge and supplies were shared between the members, and beers made at home began to improve. Often, future professional brewers got their start by learning their craft on kitchen stoves or on rudimentary systems concocted from scrap metal. The undercurrent continued to grow, and four people played huge roles in shifting the mindset of what beer could be, forever changing America's brewing landscape.

Charlie Papazian wrote a book on beer making called *The Joy of Homebrewing* in 1976. Shortly thereafter, he and Charlie Matzen cofounded a group called the American Homebrewers Association, weeks after President Carter legalized homebrewing. In the process, the fledgling organization created *Zymurgy*, a magazine dedicated to homebrewing. Papazian updated his book in 1984 and republished it as *The Complete*

Joy of Homebrewing, which went on to sell over a million copies, grooming generations of future brewers.

Noted British beer author Michael Jackson became the voice of fine beer, making a career of traveling the world and writing about what he drank. If Jackson said a beer was good, it was better than any form of paid advertising. In 1977, the iconic Jackson published *The World Guide to Beer*, becoming a respected voice for all things beer.

Professionally, two men altered the future of commercial beer. In late 1976, Jack McAuliffe created New Albion Brewing Company in Sonoma, California, considered by many to be the first microbrewery in the United States. Built on a small budget, the tiny brewery didn't have the financial backing to make a lasting effort and closed after a few years. Another Californian named Ken Grossman had a much more lasting effect on the brewing world.

Based in Chico, Grossman operated on a shoestring budget, and only his grit and ingenuity enabled him to craft his small Sierra Nevada Brewing Company slowly into the brewing giant it is today. Today, over seven thousand breweries of all sizes operate in the United States, and the numbers continue to rise. Every one of these breweries has Grossman and McAuliffe to thank for paving the way.

Brewing Returns to Arizona

When Prohibition ended in 1933, a lot of alcohol-related laws were hastily put on the books, most with the intention of eliminating the criminal element that was so pervasive during Prohibition. Lawmakers simply didn't have the foresight at the time to consider a future brewing landscape that would include microbreweries, brewpubs and nanobreweries. As such, laws had to be changed before small-scale professional brewing could become reality in Arizona.

A couple local beer enthusiasts named Jerry Gantt and Sam Ciatu took it upon themselves to lobby for Arizona beer law change. Gantt, a bartender at Turf Paradise in Phoenix, wanted to see brewpubs become legal, while lawyer Ciatu wanted to legalize microbreweries. The two worked independently, and soon thereafter bills passed through the Arizona State Legislature legalizing both concepts.

BANDERSNATCH BREWPUB

"Electric" Dave Harvan became the recipient of Arizona's first microbrew license, allowing him to open Dave's Electric Brewery in Bisbee in 1988. Around the same time, the state's first brewpub, Bandersnatch Brewpub, opened in Tempe under the direction of Joe Risi and Joe and Addie Mocca.

Originally a British-influenced restaurant, the brewing business operated under the name Christopher Joseph Brewing Company. Cardinal Pale Ale and Bandersnatch Milk Stout soon became fan favorites under original brewmaster Rick Desmarais. Having been integral in the law change that allowed Bandersnatch to become a reality, Jerry Gantt was offered an opportunity to brew professionally, learning under Desmarais as a part-time assistant.

After a short time, Gantt left the brew team, replaced by Clark Nelson. Nelson spent a few years with Bandersnatch, and when he left, Gantt returned to his former post. In 1995, Gantt left for good to open Copper Canyon Brewing, with Joe Bob Grisham taking over as Bandersnatch's head brewer. Grisham turned the brewery from an extract brewery into an all-grain brewery, the approach most commercial breweries employ today.

Bandersnatch enjoyed popularity until two roadblocks changed its fortunes. First, a Tempe smoking ban prompted smokers to visit establishments that still allowed smoking, which Bandersnatch did not. Then, a City of Tempe Downtown Redevelopment Plan threatened to potentially eliminate the business altogether. Fearing the city might seize the property through eminent domain, the Moccas sold the business in 2003. The new owners eliminated the brewery, keeping the restaurant open for about four years under different names until its final closure in November 2007.

BARLEY'S BREW PUB/COYOTE SPRINGS

Joe Risi left Bandersnatch to open Barley's Brew Pub at 20th Street and Camelback in Phoenix, and Barley's won the Best Brewpub award from the *New Times* in 1990. Risi, however, wasn't long for this endeavor either.

Risi sold Barley's in 1992 to former banker Bill Garrard, who renamed it Coyote Springs Brewing Company and Café. Garrard hired Clark Nelson as brewer.

Coyote Springs' legacy in Phoenix brewing lore was less about what it accomplished and more about what it spawned. Establishing himself as a fine brewer, Nelson trained apprentice Brian Miller, who eventually succeeded him as brewer. This was not before Nelson trained another aspiring brewer named Andy Ingram, a former ASU football player who had a passion for making beer.

Nelson spent many hours brewing, mentoring and contemplating brewery ownership. Ingram was a quick study, and the two got along well. Nelson and Ingram began to discuss the idea of opening a place of their own and soon after connected with an energetic group of young entrepreneurs who were, likewise, looking to create a new brewery in Tempe.

Originally operating under the working name of Cactus Creek Brewing, the project moved forward under the name Four Peaks, with Nelson slated to be the brewer. He agreed to take the position only if he could bring his friend and mentoree Ingram. The others agreed, and Nelson handed the Coyote Springs brewing reins over to Miller and began to prepare for his new role as brewer of what would become Four Peaks Brewing Company. However, Nelson left before Four Peaks opened, founding the short-lived Steve & Clark's Brew Pub, while Ingram became the Four Peaks brewer.

Bill Garrard wanted to expand his footprint in the valley by planning to open several new locations, the first of which appeared in downtown Phoenix.

Python Pale Ale. Contract brewed for Alice Cooper'stown.

Believing the new baseball ballpark being built would revitalize the area, Garrard wanted to get in on the action.

Other breweries and restaurants followed suit, including Tommyknocker, Leinenkugel's and a new restaurant concept from shock rocker Alice Cooper called Cooper'stown. While it wasn't a brewery, Cooper'stown was a destination place restaurant that did have a few house beers contract brewed, including its popular Python Pale Ale.

The downtown Coyote Springs location did not fare nearly as well as the original location. Draining the company's finances, the lack of success downtown caused the shuttering of both locations in late 1999.

Cave Creek Chili Beer

Cave Creek Chili Beer. *Courtesy of Ed Chilleen.*

"Crazy" Ed Chilleen was a restaurateur with a lot of big ideas. Operator of the Satisfied Frog restaurant in Cave Creek, Chilleen wanted to capitalize on the growing interest in microbrewed beers, opening Black Mountain Brewing Company right next door to the Frog.

A revolutionary idea that would gain Chilleen worldwide recognition was creating a beer made with a fiery pepper. Placing a serrano pepper in each bottle provided both a conversation starter and a spicy kick, prompting Cave Creek Chili Beer to become an overnight sensation shortly after its 1991 release.

As popularity of Chili Beer continued to rise, Chilleen had the beer contract brewed to meet the growing demand that would eventually include all fifty states and Japan. Chili Beer put the Arizona brewing scene on the map.

The beer continued to be an Arizona tradition through 2017, when Cervezaria Mexicali, the Tecate, Mexico–based brewery that produced the beer, was acquired by a conglomerate and ceased production of Cave Creek Chili Beer.

McFarlane Brewing Company

Peter McFarlane and his brother Stephen opened McFarlane Brewing Company to much fanfare in 1996. The $1 million brewery spared no expense, focusing on British- and German-style beers. It became the first official microbrewery to operate in Phoenix, located on 29th Street near the 202. A twenty-barrel system ensured the brewery would be able to produce enough beer to distribute throughout the entire state.

The hefeweizen gained popularity, accounting for almost half of the brewery's total sales. In 1997, McFarlane was awarded "Best Local Brewery" by the *New Times.*

Distribution turned out to be the divisive factor that led to an unamicable split between the McFarlane brothers, ultimately leading to Stephen's departure just six months after the brewery's opening. Peter's wife, Jane, took an active role in the brewery upon Stephen's departure.

Success was short-lived for the brewery. The McFarlanes filed for bankruptcy protection and sold the brewery in the winter of 1998 to the Uptown Brewing Company. Peter became the brewer at Hops! in Scottsdale.

TOMMYKNOCKER

The Idaho Springs, Colorado company saw all sorts of opportunity with downtown Phoenix's redevelopment around the ballpark. Deciding to make a significant investment in a Phoenix brewery, Tommyknocker Brewing Company built a $3 million brewery containing a fifty-barrel brewhouse, making it the company's largest facility.

Opening on May 1, 2000, the vast brewery made quite an initial splash. The brewery had a thirty-thousand-barrel yearly capacity, and the restaurant could comfortably seat 175. Just a block away from the new ballpark, Tommyknocker instantly became the talk of the Phoenix brewing scene.

As so many others in the newly developed downtown area experienced, long-term success was not meant to be. Just two years after opening with huge expectations, Tommyknocker closed its Phoenix brewery in May 2002.

RIO SALADO

Former Deschutes brewer Tim Gossack opened Rio Salado Brewing in July 1998, located in the same Tempe warehouse that previously housed Seidmann Brewing, a brewery that shuttered its doors after just one year in existence. Adding a bottling line and a taproom with a U-shaped bar gave the space a new purpose. The brewery doubled as a live music venue.

Charlie Billingsley came on board as brewer in May 2000, leaving Arizona Roadhouse. Earlier that year, Ted Golden became sales manager for the brewery and increased the brewery's local presence in short order. He continued in that role until June 2001, when he became "beer traffic controller" at Four Peaks, a move that would propel Four Peaks to new heights.

In 2002, Gossack opened a second location in Tempe, in the heart of the Mill Avenue district, called the Salt River Saloon. This locale featured Rio Salado's beers and a vibrant live music scene with nightly live entertainment.

Years of hard work for modest profits eventually caused Gossack to become disillusioned with the brewery business. He closed the Salt River Saloon in 2005 and put the brewery up for sale. Four Peaks showed an initial interest, but when it was discovered that proper permits for the taproom were never acquired, the taproom shut down and the deal was off. Gossack closed Rio Salado Brewing in January 2006.

While it marked the end of Rio Salado, it didn't signify the end of brewing in this locale. Years later, a new eponymously named startup brewery founded by Jeff and Leah Huss opened, skyrocketing to popularity quickly, on its way to becoming a Phoenix brewing powerhouse.

PINNACLE PEAK/SONORAN BREWING COMPANY

Restaurateur Harvey McElhannon successfully ran Pinnacle Peak Patio for years but wanted in on the microbrew craze. He had a beer contract brewed for his restaurant and named it Diamondback Pale Ale, which started quite the local controversy. After McElhannon filed an application for trademark exactly one day after it was announced the new baseball team would be named the Diamondbacks, a battle over the name broke out.

As development progressed around the new stadium, which included a brewery to be named Diamondback Brewery, McElhannon relented and gave up claim to the Diamondback name, despite insisting the name was chosen long before the baseball team's official announcement.

Renaming his beer Pinnacle Peak Beer, McElhannon brought brewing operations in house, naming John Ritter head brewer. Ritter subsequently hired former Alaskan Brewing Company brewer Jim Roper to be his assistant. Ritter got the brewery up and running, and when it opened in March 1998, Roper took over as head brewer.

Pinnacle Peak had short-lived success as a brewpub until Roper left to join the rapidly growing Four Peaks in May 2002. The company continued on solely as a restaurant with a house beer contract brewed by Sonoran Brewing Company, under the direction of Scott Yarosh.

Yarosh used the dormant Pinnacle Peak brewery to produce the restaurant's house beers as well as his own Sonoran beers for distribution.

This arrangement went on for years. Eventually, Yarosh took on a partner in the brewing venture named Zach Schroeder. The two began to look for a new facility for brewing Sonoran's beers. In January 2009, a third partner, Layrd Mahler, joined the group and headed up sales and marketing for Sonoran.

The team saw growth, but their visions did not align. Just six months later, Yarosh exited the partnership.

LEINENKUGEL'S BALLPARK BREWERY

In October 1995, Phoenix's new baseball team signed a lucrative sponsorship agreement with Miller Brewing Company. One of the stipulations was that Miller would control the brewpub that was going to be located just outside the ballpark. Since Leinenkugel's, the Chippewa Falls, Wisconsin brewery, had been part of the Miller portfolio since 1988, it was a natural tenant to occupy the brewery space at the ballyard. Leinenkugel's Ballyard Brewery became the ballpark's new brewery.

Leinenkugel's Ballyard Brewery at Bank One Ballpark.

Located just west of the main gate, the freestanding red brick facility made it easy for fans to enjoy some grub and suds just steps from the ballpark. With so many midwestern transplants taking up residence in Arizona, the brewery was a home run.

Original head brewer Chris Swersey left in July 2000 and was replaced with Peter McFarlane. In February 2001, Leinenkugel's sold the restaurant portion of the business to Hi-Tops of Chicago. An iconic sports bar in Chicago, Hi-Tops wanted an outpost in Phoenix. Leinenkugel's maintained control of the brewery, creating two independent businesses under one roof. Because the businesses were separate entities, liquor laws dictated that the beer brewed within the facility had to be sold back to the restaurant.

Establishments within a mile radius of the ballpark had packed houses on game days, but when the team wasn't playing, it was an entirely different story. Many hotspots sat mostly empty, while the cost of rent remained high.

Hi-Tops eventually sold to restaurant chain McFadden's, which purchased less and less Leinenkugel beers, reducing brewery profitability. With prospects bleak, the Leinenkugel Ballyard Brewery closed in December 2003, and McFarlane relocated to Portland, Oregon, to work for Rogue Brewery.

Gordon Biersch Brewery

Gordon Biersch Brewery is the brainchild of Californians Dan Gordon and Dean Biersch. Gordon spent time working for brewing behemoth Anheuser-Busch and later graduated from the prestigious Technical University of Munich, completing a rigorous five-year program. Biersch had his own extensive résumé in restaurant management, making the two a perfect fit to form a business.

Aggressively opening locations, Gordon Biersch entered Arizona by establishing a prime location in the heart of Arizona State country on the corner of Mill Avenue and 5th Street in Tempe in July 1998. Gordon Biersch produced mostly German-style beers, with the flavorful Oktoberfest-style marzen being exceptionally popular. Gordon Biersch has since opened several locations around Phoenix, although the original location in Tempe closed permanently in July 2019, just months after the Scottsdale location also shuttered. Locations in Glendale and Gilbert remain open, still as popular as ever.

Rock Bottom

Gordon Biersch wasn't the only chain brewpub finding success in the valley. Founded in 1991 in Denver, Colorado, Rock Bottom was growing rapidly. The name spawned from the original brewery being located at the bottom of the Prudential Building—known as "The Rock"—thus the name *Rock Bottom*.

The company entered the Arizona market by opening its first area location in Ahwatukee on March 29, 1999. It wouldn't be long before the brewpub chain would expand locally. On July 1, 2001, the company purchased the Scottsdale Hops! and Glendale Cougan's locations, creating two new Rock Bottom locations in the valley. In November 2001, the fourth location opened in the newly created Desert Ridge complex in northern Phoenix, with Brian Helton relocating from the Cincinnati Rock Bottom location to become the head brewer.

In late 2010, Gordon Biersch and Rock Bottom merged to form a new company known as CraftWorks Restaurants and Breweries Inc. Along with a third concept known as Old Chicago, the company now has upward of two hundred locations nationwide owned or franchised.

The Unlikely Cowboy

The year 2002 saw the opening of a new brewery in Scottsdale's DC Ranch called the Unlikely Cowboy. Ryan Ashley was the well-trained brains behind the operation, having spent time studying at Siebel, Doemens Brewing Academy and UC Davis, three brewing school powerhouses. As his grandfather worked for Miller Brewing, beer was in the family's blood.

Ashley relocated to Arizona from Libertyville, Illinois, where he brewed with Chris Swersey at Mickey Finn's Brewery. Swersey also relocated to Arizona to become Leinenkugel's Ballpark Brewery's first brewmaster. Ashley opened Unlikely Cowboy with his two brothers, and the brewpub featured an extensive menu to complement his award-winning beers. After picking up a medal at the Great American Beer Festival in 2003, Ashley renamed his brewpub the Cowboy.

Despite the quality of his beers, Ashley was fighting a losing battle competing against top-flight chains in the exclusive Market Street area. Trying to generate a spark, Ashley again renamed his brewery Zona Brewing Company in 2004. When that didn't turn things around, Zona Brewing closed in November 2005.

Old World Brewery

In the fall of 2007, Patrick Fields began to publicize a new concept called Old World Brewery. Wanting to get beers into the marketplace before his physical location opened, Fields worked a deal with Sonoran Brewing to contract brew his beers.

In November 2008, Fields took on partner Perry Parmely, who became the company's president. Matt Mercer was next to join, becoming the head brewer. Opening in a warehouse located near Deer Valley Airport, Old World opened to the public on January 24, 2009.

The partners, who were also musicians, designed Old World to be both a brewery and music venue. The hot spot featured live music regularly until a conflict with the landlord led to termination of the lease agreement.

In July 2010, with the help of new investor Jeff Olson, Old World started the relocation process to the former Capital Station post office building in Phoenix. During the interim, Fields had its beers contract brewed by Mogollon Brewing in Flagstaff. Relocation did not save the young brewery, which eventually closed its doors for good.

Dave's Electric Brewpub

Wanting to capitalize on "Electric" Dave Harvan's popular Bisbee-based beer, Dave Hoffman and Scott Burge created an agreement with Harvan to create a brewpub in Tempe that would showcase Harvan's beers. Located near the Mill Avenue entertainment district, the venue was entirely Hoffman and Burge's undertaking, with Harvan's only responsibility to provide the beer as an independent contractor.

The new brewpub was set to open in September 2009, but Harvan was involved in a serious car accident. Without the brewer to produce the beers, the brewpub's opening was pushed back to late October. As Harvan recovered, the brewpub opened for a trial run in October, with the official grand opening taking place on November 19, 2009.

Until the brewhouse could be built in Tempe, all the beer came from Electric Dave's in Bisbee, brewed by Harvan's assistant Caleb Johnson as Harvan recovered. By February 2011, the brewpub was finally producing its own beer. A recovered Harvan and Johnson commuted to and from Bisbee on brew days.

This arrangement ended when Hoffman and Burge decided to go in another direction, changing the name to Mad Hatter Brewpub in April 2012, cutting ties with Harvan. Unsuccessful, the brewpub closed for good just seven months later.

SLEEPY DOG BREWERY

Sleepy Dog Saloon and Brewery was opened in Tempe in November 2009 by Robert Sizemore and Debbie Conforti. Sizemore was a homebrewer who interned briefly under Brian Helton at Rock Bottom. With the help of assistant brewer Matt Weber, the dog-themed beers began to grow in popularity.

Eventually, the brewery was acquired by Two Brothers Brewing, an Illinois-based brewery that opened a satellite brewpub in Scottsdale not long before the acquisition. Under Two Brothers direction, Sleepy Dog continues to operate to this day.

THE FLEETING BREWERY SCENE

Countless factors can contribute to the success or failure of a business. Restaurant-related businesses are known for being some of the riskiest entrepreneurial endeavors. High closures were a consistent theme during this time in the Phoenix brewing scene.

Whether it was timing, improper funding, lack of business experience or otherwise, many businesses came and went during the decades that preceded the Phoenix brewery rush of the 2010s. Businesses such as Hops Bistro, Tombstone Brewing, Copper Canyon, Uptown Brewing, Arizona Roadhouse and Steve & Clark's all experienced some levels of success before ultimately closing their doors for good. While it may have signaled the end for these businesses, it was just the start for a brewing scene that was about to explode.

4

THE RISE OF FOUR PEAKS BREWING COMPANY

Andy Ingram had big dreams early in life. Owning Arizona's most successful brewery was not one of them. In fact, the beer world wasn't anywhere on Ingram's list of life goals. His dreams were on the football field. As a tight end on full scholarship for the Arizona State football team, Ingram had hopes of a possible career in the NFL. Injuries cut his football career short, and the subsequent surgeries forced him to shift gears. Devastated by having to give up football, Ingram decided to spend a year as an exchange student. He traveled to London to study during his fourth year of college, working toward a degree in psychology.

Though Ingram had only a lukewarm interest in beer, his time in London introduced him to the common pubs of London. They had an entirely different look and feel from the raucous college bars of Arizona State, and he developed an interest in the pub culture of England.

After his year was up, he returned to ASU to complete his psychology degree, which he earned at the conclusion of his fifth collegiate year. His plan was to take the summer off and then attend grad school.

A friend's dad had a homebrewing setup that Ingram and his friend used to learn how to brew. Making mostly English ales, Ingram caught the brewing bug almost immediately. Wanting to hone his skills and learn whatever he could, his newfound passion led him to Clark Nelson, the brewer at Coyote Springs Brewing Company of Phoenix. Nelson was a full-time mailman who brewed at Coyote Springs in his spare time.

Andy Ingram, brewmaster, Four Peaks.

With a change in his mail delivery schedule, Nelson was unable to meet the demands of both his day job and the brewery. He asked Ingram if he'd be interested in assisting him at the brewery, part time. As a college student in need of a few dollars, Ingram jumped at the chance because it meant income while gaining additional brewing knowledge.

Part-time quickly became full-time at Coyote Springs, where the excessive workload honed Ingram's skills in a hurry. He realized how much he enjoyed making beer professionally. This discovery made him reconsider a life in the field of psychology, and he dropped plans to attend grad school.

Ingram learned from Nelson and honed his craft through trial and error. The beers at Coyote Springs developed a following, many of which were crafted in the English style that Ingram came to love during his time in London.

Both Nelson and Ingram had visions of creating a brewery of their own, rather than toiling long hours for someone else. The two put together a business plan.

On the periphery was another group of four guys who had similar visions but different backgrounds. The group consisted of David Roberts, John "Vegas" Hostak, Walter Geerdts and Jim Scussel. The foursome had some background in finance and business organization, but not much in the way of brewing knowledge. When the two groups crossed paths, they realized they had complementary skills that could be well served by partnering together.

After exhausting all traditional options for raising money to no avail, the group had to get creative.

Dave Roberts went to visit his uncle who owned a cider company in England. During that visit, an unexpected opportunity arose. They visited the Bass Brewery, where they saw a huge field of unused short and stout serving vessels known as Grundy tanks. These tanks can be used to ferment and/or serve beer. Roberts learned Bass had to remove them all from its pubs due to a powerful movement in the UK known as CAMRA, the campaign for real ale, which decreed beer should be served from casks rather than serving tanks.

Since the tanks were sitting in storage at Bass Brewery, Roberts inquired about purchasing them. Bass was more than willing to get rid of them, and a new partnership was established. The group created an unexpected new source of income.

While opening a brewery was still the plan, a beer tank resale company is what came first. Importing Grundy tanks by the container load, the first shipment went straight to a series of Northwest brewpubs known as McMenamins, immediately establishing this group of young Tempe entrepreneurs as a reliable source for reasonably priced brewing equipment. The group began advertising these tanks for sale in brewing magazines, resulting in consistent demand.

When all was said and done, the future brewing company imported almost 1,400 units and sold all but 29 of them, keeping those for future use. The margins were significant, and this unexpected source of revenue provided most of the startup funds to get the brewery project off the ground. Incidentally, the 29 Grundy tanks are still in use today.

While Clark Nelson left to pursue other endeavors, Dave Roberts found a long vacant building on 8th Street that would eventually serve as the brewery's iconic location. Heavy with history, the building had been an icehouse, dairy creamery and recording studio but most recently housed a Chinese food importer/exporter. Extensive work was needed to turn this dilapidated building into a functional brewery.

Undeterred, the team got to work. Demolition alone took six months. As they hauled away garbage and pulled down the drop ceiling, they discovered the building had a beautiful ceiling surrounded by red brick walls previously hidden. The more the team worked, the more they uncovered a hidden gem. On a shoestring budget, they did the majority of the work themselves.

During the process, they found out the building was on the fire department's "do not enter" list. This meant if a fire were to break out, the fire department was under orders to let the building burn. As they needed to install a full sprinkler system to get up to code, the budget took another hit. Such is life opening a new brewery.

It took about eighteen months to turn the building into an operational brewery. The days of the towering 240-barrel tanks were far in the future. Prototype batches were brewed on a modest-sized Brew Magic System, producing just ten gallons at a time.

Façade of Four Peaks' 8th Street Brewery. *Courtesy of Four Peaks.*

The business needed an official name. A working name had been "Cactus Creek Brewing Company," which Andy is famous for saying "sounds like a retirement home." Clearly not sold on the name, the group gathered around a whiteboard brainstorming names. Then, each member put his favorite four names on a ballot, ranked in order of preference. While no one had Four Peaks listed as his favorite, it was the only name to appear on each ballot. Very marketable for the region, the new business finally had its name.

Being influenced by his earlier trip to England, Ingram gravitated toward English ale styles. That tendency was reinforced when Ingram met Barry John, a veteran brewer formerly with Young's Brewery of England. John helped Ingram formulate recipes during the brewery's infancy. Ingram embraced John's English style of brewing, which fit the brewery's developing personality perfectly. John spent ten months unofficially mentoring Ingram, a period of time that Ingram remembers fondly.

With so many driven personalities working closely together, conflict began to arise, resulting in Roberts and Hostak exiting the group. Eventually, Roberts and Hostak relocated to Rocky Point, Mexico, opening Al Capone's Pizza.

The remaining partners settled nicely into their roles. Ingram took full control of the brewing operations. Upper Midwest transplant Jim Scussel became the de facto CFO. Scussel was the unsung hero who did a lot of the behind-the-scenes work that required long hours and intense attention to detail, such as legal, licensing, financials and overall business operations. Scussel wore many different hats simultaneously, often including marketing and sales initiatives.

As Roberts and Hostak were departing, Randy Schultz came into the fold. Arriving in the desert with not much more than his optimism and an old pickup truck, Schultz was introduced to the team through a mutual friend. With plenty of restaurant experience, he impressed the team with his willingness to jump in and do whatever was needed. His arrival was timely, since the partners envisioned opening a restaurant as the natural evolution of their brewery. Schultz joined them and immediately immersed himself into the planning of the restaurant.

Four Peaks' 8th Street bar. *Courtesy of Four Peaks.*

Though Four Peaks started out as solely a production brewery, the restaurant came to fruition about three years into the company's existence. Randy eventually became the front of house manager when the final piece of the partner puzzle, Arthur Craft, came on board to handle all kitchen duties.

A native Arizonan, Craft was a Chaparral High School graduate who went on to study at New York's prestigious Culinary Institute of America. A quiet introvert, Craft instantly brought credentials to the aspiring new brewpub without the flair that often accompanies accomplished chefs. With a menu that reflected a gastropub-type experience, the Four Peaks brewpub far exceeded expectations of most patrons expecting standard bar fare.

It was angel investor Dan MacBeth who made the transition from production brewery to full-service brewpub possible. MacBeth initially envisioned opening a brewpub of his own, but it never came to fruition. Instead, as he approached his retirement years, he invested in the potential of Four Peaks as a silent investor. Never intending to be an active partner in the business, MacBeth was extremely instrumental in building out the kitchen and brewpub area.

Working hard, making the sacrifices necessary to succeed, the partners did not take paychecks for the first year of the company's existence. Ingram waited tables in what little spare time he had to ensure he could pay his house payment.

Success began to build, then snowball. With double-digit growth year after year, Four Peaks began to establish itself as a household name in Phoenix. Its brands were appearing in more and more establishments around town, and the brewpub on 8th Street in Tempe became *the* place to be.

While the partners shouldered the work themselves early on, soon it became necessary to expand the staff. Needing brewhouse help, Andy hired a local homebrew supply worker named Anthony Canecchia to be a part-time kegger. He worked his way up to become a brewer.

With demand growing, Charlie Billingsley, formerly of Rock Bottom Brewery, came on board and was responsible for setting up the brewery's quality assurance program. Ingram also hired brewer Jim Roper. Having brewed at the respected Alaskan Brewing Company during a huge growth phase, Roper helped Alaskan become a national player.

Roper relocated to Arizona, taking a job as a one-man brewing operation for Pinnacle Peak Brewing before connecting with Ingram and becoming a Four Peaks brewer.

The gastropub experience of Four Peaks. *Courtesy of Four Peaks.*

After Canecchia was let go after six years, he founded SanTan Brewing Company of Chandler, Arizona, which has gone on to become Arizona's second-largest brewer. Meanwhile, Roper worked his way up to the position of head of brewing operations.

Ted Golden joined the company in the early 2000s to help expand the Four Peaks footprint into the marketplace. Golden came from Rio Salado Brewing and was formerly of Budweiser, where he worked in sales for the mega beer conglomerate. Distributing mostly draft beer, Golden hit the pavement hard and grew the brand significantly.

Eventually, he hired his own staff, becoming national sales director. As the company increased its bottle/can production, placements became increasingly more common in stores, restaurants, bars and entertainment facilities. Four Peaks went from startup to a craft beer force in a relatively short period of time.

Hensley Distributing also played an integral role in the brand growing as quickly as it did. Acquiring the brand from Alliance beverage in 2009, Hensley hit the market with full force, supporting Golden's efforts. Making Four Peaks part of every conversation, Hensley placed beers in every location possible. Being a Budweiser distributor, Hensley was used to moving a lot of product and making strategic, high-profile placements. The brewery and the distributor made a perfect pair, having a great deal of success together to this day. With Hensley's help, Four Peaks not only got placed in the major national grocery retailers but also appeared in huge venues such as the Phoenix Suns basketball arena and the Arizona Cardinals football stadium.

Four Peaks beers were consistent and quickly developed a following. 8th Street Pale Ale was an early favorite, a balanced pale ale that invoked both English and American craft beer influences. Just over 5% ABV and moderately hoppy, 8th Street has an easy drinking palate that finishes crisp, making it a fine pairing with many dishes.

Sunbru was a nod to partner Jim Scussel's love for German-style brews, made in the Kolsch style. Very light in color and body, Sunbru is the perfect beer to transition a macrobrew drinker into craft. The beer was named in tribute to the defunct Arizona Brewing Company, which produced a beer of the same name many years earlier. It was a symbolic passing of the baton, tying a bit of history into this ever-growing brewery.

Hop Knot IPA capitalized on the growing popularity of the IPA style, combining a solid backbone of bready malt flavor along with an upfront, yet restrained, clean hop flavor. A stronger offering at 6.7% ABV, it was still very approachable. The Peach Ale was crafted as a golden ale made with an infusion of peaches. With flavorful peach essence, the 4.5% ABV Peach Ale became the ultimate pool-side refresher.

There was another beer initially called Four Peaks Scottish Amber that made a splash in more ways than one. Initially brewed as a strong "Scotch" ale, the beer packed a wallop. One evening, Ingram thanked the construction crew by tapping a keg of this brew and letting them enjoy it at their leisure. All he asked for in return was a little feedback about the beer. Ingram arrived the next day to find the worksite empty. The beer was quite a bit stronger than originally anticipated, and the workers needed a little recovery time. Lesson learned, Ingram recrafted a lighter, more approachable 6% ABV version of the style.

The team knew they had a winner with this reworked Scottish-style amber, though they never could have expected the meteoric rise it would soon enjoy. Considering the hot, dry climate, no one could have predicted a malt-forward, 6% ABV beer would become an Arizona staple. Four Peaks Scottish Amber was relatively popular under its original name, but it didn't stand out from the rest of the Four Peaks offerings. A name change altered its fortunes dramatically.

One sunny afternoon, Dan MacBeth and the other partners gathered at a local Scottsdale watering hole that was having a talent show open to patrons. Dressed in Scottish attire, equipped with a kilt, the sixty-something-year-old MacBeth decided to participate. He got up on stage, danced a jig and finished his act by lifting his kilt to the shock of the crowd. It caused quite a reaction from friends and audience alike. MacBeth had become the kilt lifter. A seed was planted, and it spawned an idea.

The brain trust decided that the idea needed to live on. They renamed their Scottish-style ale "Kilt Lifter," and a legend was born.

Kilt Lifter is currently the most popular beer crafted in the state of Arizona. Over 60 percent of the beer produced by Four Peaks is Kilt Lifter alone.

Four Peaks also capitalized on the seasonal beer market. Putting a unique spin on the growing popularity of the pumpkin beer market, Ingram and his team took a traditional porter recipe and added real pumpkins that were first caramelized in a pizza oven. The beer became an overnight sensation and remains a popular seasonal offering to this day. They no longer use real pumpkins due to the late harvest, instead using a high-quality pumpkin puree in order to meet the seasonal demand.

Kilt Lifter, the most popular beer brewed in Arizona. *Courtesy of Four Peaks.*

The beers of Four Peaks have won countless awards on some of the world's biggest stages. Kilt Lifter has been a multiple award winner, earning five Great American Beer Festival medals and two World Beer Cup awards.

Ingram's attention to making solid, consistent beers coupled with Golden's relentless pavement pounding resulted in more and more business. Four Peaks' popularity found them reaching capacity at their current location, and expansion became a necessity. Because they were now an established, successful company, banks were willing to loan money, unlike in the early startup days. They received a substantial bank loan, which prompted planning for a new facility on Wilson Avenue in Tempe that would significantly increase production capabilities.

The group envisioned distribution outside Arizona. The group bet on the future and designed a brewery that could produce 150,000 barrels of beer per year. The Wilson location is almost sixty thousand square feet of space with a state-of-the-art bottling line and brewhouse. The Wilson facility opened in October 2013.

Armed with a brand-new brewery capable of producing huge amounts of beer, the team considered ways of expanding their footprint beyond their well-established Arizona turf. Knowing the company would need help both strategically and monetarily if it was ever going to expand regionally or nationally, the partners began to look for outside opportunities to take their business to the next level. The time had also come to start thinking about a future succession plan. They decided to gauge outside interest in the brewery and hired First Beverage, well known in the industry for brokering brewery deals.

Several opportunities arose, any of which would have infused a great deal of money into the company. After weighing a few serious offers, and deciding they'd rather sell to a brewer than a venture capitalist firm, Four Peaks sold the business to Anheuser-Busch InBev.

"In the end, we wanted to be true to ourselves, so it made sense to sell to another brewer, not a venture capitalist or a bank," said Ingram. Not much has changed in the day-to-day operations of the company. "ABI told me, we're not buying you because you are broken, we're buying you because you are working well," said Ingram.

According to Ingram, the transition has been relatively smooth. The partners are still active as advisors, except for Arthur Craft, who retired after the sale. He now enjoys life boarding horses in Scottsdale. "We still have so much autonomy in everything from beer styles to business to how to run the business," said Ingram.

Four Peaks expected some backlash from the craft beer community because of the sale to the mega-conglomerate, but the negative chatter was minimal. Now its beers go far beyond the borders of Arizona, and the company is enjoying acclaim throughout the country, rather than just in its own backyard.

Having ABI as a parent company has provided plenty of perks, as well. The equipment resources are virtually limitless, and the group now has access to things they've never before dreamed possible. When it was time to design a new lager, they had access to the entire databank of ABI yeast strains and were able to use a sought-after strain from the German brewer Augustiner, giving the beer a distinct flavor profile. The QA/QC team from ABI consistently ensures everything is of the utmost quality by using state-of-the-art, high-tech equipment, something a small, independent brewer simply wouldn't have the resources to accomplish.

The company started the Four Peaks Foundation to support local charities, including one of its own called Four Peaks for Teachers. With Ingram's wife being a longtime schoolteacher, the Ingrams have firsthand knowledge of the struggles many teachers face daily.

Partnering with an office supply store, the Four Peaks for Teachers event allows teachers to receive a voucher they can redeem for a box of school supplies. Teachers receive much-needed paper, pens, calculators and supplies for their classrooms. Four Peaks continues to take pride in making a difference in the community as a respected partner.

Four Peaks is named after We-Ko-Pa, a revered, spiritual Yavapai term that represents the majestic mountain range that overlooks the northeast side of the Phoenix valley. The brewery continues to rise to new peaks, rewriting Arizona brewing history, as it leads the way in an ever evolving and continuously growing craft brewing scene.

5

THE MODERN ERA OF BREWING IN PHOENIX

CENTRAL PHOENIX BREWERIES

Helio Basin

Undergrads at Allegany College in Meadville, Pennsylvania, Dustin Hazer and Mike Conley simply had a taste for good beer. Their college campus selection was less than desirable, so the pair decided that if they couldn't find what they were looking for, they should just brew it themselves. The two decided to brew a robust porter as their first beer, Hazer's personal favorite style. The beer came out great, and the friends were instantly hooked on homebrewing.

Hazer was studying microbiology and chemistry, two sciences integral to the brewing process. In an act of ingenuity and resourcefulness, they convinced the school's science department to fund their homebrewing practices for faculty picnics. The caveat was that, in an effort to advance higher learning, they had to perform biological lab testing on the beer to make it educational. The science department heads had plenty of beer for their events, while Hazer and Conley earned invaluable brewing and lab experience.

The path to brewery ownership was anything but direct. After graduation, Hazer studied pharmaceutical science in South Dakota while Conley enlisted in the Marines. Conley did tours of duty in Okinawa and Afghanistan, rising to the rank of first lieutenant.

Dustin Hazer, Helio Basin founder and brewmaster. *Courtesy of Dustin Hazer.*

During his time in South Dakota, a friend who enjoyed Hazer's beers suggested he attend professional brewing school. Inspired by the idea, Hazer left the research world and enrolled in respected brewing academy Siebel Institute of Technology. Hazer's science background got him into a class of professional brewers, of which Hazer was the only amateur.

Being around professional brewers accelerated Hazer's learning curve. With a pharmaceutical career in his rear-view mirror, Hazer graduated from Siebel and got a job at Ellicottville Brewing Company, near his small hometown in the state of New York. EBC was a perfect fit for Hazer. Its current brewer had a lot of real-life experience but no formal training. Hazer had extensive formal training but no professional experience. The complementary skill sets benefitted both brewers.

After brewing at Ellicottville for just over two years, he connected with Andy Ingram of Four Peaks Brewing. The two met in person at the craft brewer's conference that year and hit it off. Soon after, Ingram offered Hazer a job brewing for Four Peaks. Hazer saw this as an opportunity to take his skills to the next level. He accepted, relocated and brewed for Four Peaks for the next three years.

Loving the Arizona desert with no plans to go elsewhere, Hazer got a call in 2012 from Phin DeMink, owner of Southern Tier Brewing of Lakewood, New York. Having known Hazer from his time at Ellicottville, DeMink reached out to gauge if he had interest in going back east. Southern Tier had plans to build a new production facility with a state-of-the-art, German-manufactured automated brewhouse. Knowing this was another unique opportunity to increase his overall brewhouse skills, Hazer moved back to his home state of New York and went to work for DeMink at Southern Tier.

Hazer was present for the installation of the new 110-barrel system at Southern Tier. He jumped right in and took over all operations. In addition to brewing around the clock, Hazer oversaw the installation of the new brewery, working sixteen-to-eighteen-hour days to ensure a smooth brewery operation.

Southern Tier produced a respectable 40,000 barrels of beer a year before Hazer's arrival, and by the time he left four years later, the company eclipsed 100,000 barrels.

In a few short years, Hazer had created an impressive résumé. Heading up operations at a world-class brewery that produced award-winning beers would be the wildest dreams of many brewers, but Hazer thought back to the days he and his former college roommate Conley dreamed of opening a place of their own. Brewery ownership kept pulling at Hazer.

When Conley left the Marines, he enrolled at Arizona State. Throughout his travels, Hazer kept in touch with his old roommate. By that point, Hazer had accomplished all he hoped to at Southern Tier during his four-year tenure. The company was stable and thriving. If there was ever a time for Hazer to take the dive into brewery ownership, this was it.

Having fallen in love with Arizona during his time with Four Peaks, Hazer wanted to put down roots in the Copper State. Moving back to Arizona, he partnered up with Conley, and the two found property for their new brewery relatively quickly.

Conley built his business plan, met with entrepreneurs and visited many breweries. He completed a business internship with Draught Works Brewery in Missoula, Montana. He worked nights at a local Phoenix-area brewery while getting Helio Basin up and running during the day. Conley applied principles he learned in the Marines to ensure a smooth opening of the brewery.

"Transitioning from the Marines into owning a business, a lot of lessons carried over," said Conley. "Basic things such as teamwork, supporting your men/women, and continually finding solutions when unexpected problems arise. Other complex components also come into play such as holding yourself accountable for everything that happens, motivating yourself and your employees and being able to make decisions without having all the information. These are all things that are instilled into Marines and having that experience really helped me throughout every step of the way."

As Conley was forming the business, Hazer began designing the brewery's beer lineup. He took a simple approach, sticking to six core beers. After he installed a fifteen-barrel brewhouse, Helio Basin brewery opened in July 2016 with an official grand opening during the second week of August.

The best-seller is Helio Basin American IPA, an "old-school, East Coast IPA," according to Hazer. The IPA features American hop varietals such as Columbus, Cascade, Centennial, Chinook and Citra.

Right behind the IPA in popularity is 602 Brew. A very approachable light blonde ale, 602 checks in at 4.7% ABV and 18 IBU. The beer, named after the Phoenix area code, is a favorite of many local brewers who admire the clean character of this light ale.

Hazer's favorite beer in the lineup is the Helio Basin Porter. With coffee, chocolate and roast character, this robust porter was the very first beer brewed by Hazer and Conley during their college days, and the recipe remains unchanged.

Hazer handles all brewhouse duties while Conley handles the front of the house and accounting duties. Equipped with a full-service scratch restaurant featuring artisanal American classic cuisine, Helio Basin earned the "Best New Restaurant and Brewery" award from *Phoenix Magazine* in 2016. The duo also received national notoriety when *Beer Advocate* named Helio Basin one of the top thirty breweries in 2016.

While the original business plan called for producing only draft, Helio Basin began to can its beer. Doing so presented other opportunities, such as partnering with local reggae-rock outfit Fayuca on a beer called Fayuca Rizing Extra Pale Ale. Crafted specifically for the band and its fans, the 6.3% ABV, 60 IBU beer is a crushable concert thirst quencher with hints of pine, spice, grapefruit and melon.

Helio Basin embraces the Phoenix community, especially those in the local brewing community. In addition to Hazer being on the technical committee for the Arizona Brewers Guild, Helio Basin holds an annual brewers-only event, shutting down the restaurant to the public, giving hardworking brewers across the state a chance to get together and connect over some beers.

Hazer gets excited when thinking about future prospects for his brewery. "The Arizona beer scene is still young and there's plenty of room to grow."

Helton Brewing Company

Having a brewery named after himself belies the quiet, unassuming nature of Brian Helton. A lifer in the brewing industry, Helton worked in the corporate world of brewing before taking the leap of faith and going out on his own.

"I opened breweries from the ground up at my previous company, so I had plenty of experience in knowing how to build a place top-to-bottom," said Helton. "But it all started with the work ethic I learned from my father back in Indiana."

A self-proclaimed "Indiana redneck," Helton was born in Terre Haute, Indiana, and later relocated to another small Hoosier State town known as Aurora. Helton's college career took him to Cincinnati, Ohio, where he attended the University of Cincinnati. Studying environmental engineering with a strong math background, Helton was acquiring the skills he'd eventually need to own and operate a brewery. At this time, however, owning a brewery was not even a consideration.

Helton and his father built houses in Brian's teenage years, which created a strong work ethic in him. "I was stripping wire and putting in lights at age nine with my father. I always believe in trying to do things yourself if at all possible," he said.

While working to complete his degree, Helton was introduced to the Germanic-influenced beer scene of Cincinnati. Craft breweries such as Oldenberg and Barrel House showed Helton what a great brewery could be.

After graduation, Helton worked for six years as a wetland delineator until having an "aha" moment one day. He asked himself a simple question, "Is there anyone at this company with whom I would want to have a beer?" When he realized the answer was "no," it was time for some soul searching.

At age twenty-eight, Helton decided it was time to figure out what he wanted to do with the rest of his working life. Having a keen interest in cooking, he considered applying to culinary school. As it turned out, the school he applied to wouldn't even consider his application unless he had at least one year of working in the industry on his résumé. Helton searched for an opportunity to work in the industry to meet this requirement.

He contacted a friend who worked in a brewery, and the friend got him in at the bottom—as a barback. Helton didn't care what the position was, he just needed the year of experience to follow through on his culinary school plan.

Left: Brian Helton, owner/brewmaster, Helton Brewing.

Below: Helton Brewing kegs ready for market. *Courtesy of Brian Helton.*

With his natural curiosity and background in engineering and math, Helton was instinctively inquisitive and learned everything he could about beer and the brewing process. If he was going to work there, he might as well know as much as he could about the company and how it operated.

In less than six months, Helton showed an aptitude toward brewing and a willingness to expand his functionality at the brewery. He was promoted to assistant brewer and began to learn the skills and intricacies of making beer. Determined and inspired, Helton found a new path, one that no longer required enrollment in culinary school. Brian Helton had become a professional brewer.

After successfully brewing for years, Helton found himself in middle management for this corporate company, overseeing the operation of five to six regional breweries. Though successful in this role, he felt stuck in middle management with no room to grow. He wanted a change. Part of his role was installing breweries in new cities, seeing them through from conceptual idea to operating brewery, so he knew he had the knowledge and the ability to do it for himself.

It was time to leave the safe confines of corporate America and take a chance on himself. Enter Helton Brewing Company.

While Helton Brewing has about a dozen silent investors that own very small portions of the business, Brian owns 51 percent of the business and is the owner, operator and brewmaster. A hands-on leader, Helton is not afraid to dive into whatever needs to be done. With his drive and work ethic, he embarked on building his own brewery.

Knowing the landlord/tenant relationship could be a tenuous one, he wanted to ensure that when he opened his place, he could own the building outright.

He found a large building on the corner of 22nd Street and Indian School in Phoenix that had the proper zoning necessary to be able to operate a full-scale brewery. Though the building had much more space than he originally needed, he was keenly aware of the rapid growth of successful breweries. He purchased a building that gave him room for future expansion.

With Helton at the lead, he and his first employees worked together doing all they could to get the brewery built and operational, keeping external contractors to a bare minimum. Constructing, painting, running lines and setting up equipment, Helton was able to be cash positive on day one by not accruing heavy debt to contractors. Helton Brewing opened for business on May 10, 2016, making an immediate impact in the Phoenix brewing scene.

Helton Brewing beers come in all flavors and colors. *Courtesy of Brian Helton.*

On any given day, Helton may alternate between cook, floor mopper, bartender, media relations liaison and staff trainer, all while pondering the next day's brew. That's if he's not in the back brewing or constructing his very own canning line.

Unlike the majority of competitors who try to be all things to all people, Helton has a modest tap list, focusing on beers he has perfected over the years. The very first beer brewed was Helton's popular Scotch Ale, a beer that served the double duty of propagating his yeast bank for other brews.

Spending many formative years in Cincinnati, a city with a strong German heritage, Helton developed a true appreciation for classic styles of beers such as pilsner and marzen. Understanding the nuances of beers like pilsner, he honed his palate early on and learned to identify and understand off flavors—a skill he perfected over the years. The ability to brew a perfectly clean lager can separate a good brewer from a great one, and Helton took the time to master the necessary skills.

Valley Venom Pilsner is a year-round staple on draft and one of the finest, cleanest beers made in Arizona. Using a simple recipe of pilsner malt, Saaz hops and clean German lager yeast, the unfiltered pilsner is brilliantly clear, crisp and refreshing. The fall seasonal, known as Dark German Lager, is a flavorful, traditional lager made in the marzen style. The Scotch Ale pleases those looking for a richer, caramelized malt-forward ale, while the hoppy Northeast IPA has become the brewery's number-one seller at the time of this writing.

Running a brewing facility does not allow much time for introspection, but there was one moment when Helton realized he had accomplished something great.

"When I realized four or five other breweries were buying our pilsner and putting it on tap at their establishment, that was the ultimate testament to the quality of our product. It was a pretty cool thing to experience," he said.

Helton is on a mission to be an integral part of a still-growing craft beer scene that he sees going in the right direction:

> *I had heard that certain states were colonizing Arizona, saying that there were 5.2 million people who lacked good local beer and needed to be satisfied through out-of-state breweries. These breweries were trying to establish themselves in our market....I am so proud to take back our state by being of one many breweries coming to the table with solid beers. Our local beer industry works collaboratively especially when it comes to resources and knowledge sharing. We're doing more collaboration beers now than ever before and the quality is at an all-time high. It's fun to be part of such a great community.*

The mission at Helton Brewing Company is to be innovative while still respecting the purity of the craft.

"We always want to pay homage to the history because that's what got us here," he affirmed. "I love to share my knowledge with other brewers because others did the same for me when I was just starting out. The brewing community is a brother and sisterhood that makes you feel you are a part of something greater than yourself. These allies will never let you fail; they will help you in any way they can and that makes me feel like I have a safety net to fall back on."

He looks for people with a similar passion for craft beer because the passion shows in their work. "I try to surround myself with people that are wiser and more knowledgeable than me because it makes me better," he admitted.

The beer industry has its peaks and valleys and has a way of changing a person's outlook over time. "Being a brewmaster and having the artistic license to develop your beers and watch people enjoy them is an incredible feeling," Helton shared. But success certainly didn't happen overnight.

> *In the first one to three years, your ego gets inflated and you begin to think you're better than you are. From years three to five you start to dive deeper into brewing knowledge and begin to believe you don't know what you're*

doing. Years five to twelve you study like hell trying to learn every last thing you can possibly know about your craft. Then from years twelve to twenty, you use that knowledge and begin to see positive, repeatable results from all those years of studying through trial and error. Finally, once you've amassed twenty years in the business, you finally feel like you just might know what you're doing.

Giving back is part of the Helton Brewing Company fabric. Community-focused charitable events occur regularly. On one particular Saturday afternoon, a painting class, a brewery bus tour and a dog-friendly event on the patio happened simultaneously, packing the house. It showcased how, in the matter of just two years, this brewery has become a focal point of the local neighborhood. People of all backgrounds, income levels and walks of life sit together on the bright yellow chairs and get to know each other.

Over the years, Brian Helton has shared his knowledge with dozens of brewers looking to hone their craft and make their marks in the industry. He's enjoyed every minute of it and is happy to have been able to help others.

"I love to teach," said Helton. "My greatest moments of happiness are when one of my young brewers walks across the stage at a beer festival to accept his or her medal for making an award-winning beer. That's when I know I've done my job. You have to have a passion for this industry to be part of it and that's what makes it so much fun," he says.

Helton Brewing taproom.

Mother Bunch Brewing

Female brewery ownership may be more prevalent today, but it was rare when Julie Meeker first got involved in the industry. Brewing on her stovetop before upgrading to all-grain batches, the Rockville, Maryland native got the brewing bug in the early 1990s when craft breweries were just starting to enter the mainstream.

A founding member of Girls Pint Out, a group for women wanting to expand their knowledge of beer, Meeker knew she wanted to be involved in the brewing industry in some capacity. Having worked in construction for twenty-five years, she was ready for change. She wrote a business plan in 2003 to open a hop farm in southwestern Arizona. Coming to realize Arizona wasn't an ideal location for growing hops, she wrote another business plan, this time for a brewpub.

Like most people who dream of opening breweries, Meeker didn't have the deep pockets needed to initially make it happen. Determined to make this dream a reality, she put up about half the money herself and worked with the small business development center at Gateway Community College, which helped her secure a bank loan.

"I was researching alewives and came across a seventeenth-century jest book called *Pasquils Jests Mixed with Mother Bunches Merriments*," said Meeker. "Mother Bunch was a character in the stories. It's my nod back to women and brewing."

Regularly patronizing Four Peaks Brewing Company in Tempe paid dividends when Meeker ended up with some of Four Peaks' original brewing equipment as it upgraded to larger vessels. With help from local brewing veteran Jerry Gantt, they got the brewery set up.

"Jerry took a liking to me when I first joined the guild and wanted to open a brewery," said Meeker. Mother Bunch Brewing opened on September 15, 2014.

When the original brewer didn't work out, Gantt agreed to come on board as a working consultant, solidifying the brewing operations.

Chef Holly Arguello was on board even before a location was finalized. It took almost two years to find the right spot. "We lucked out with this historic building," said Meeker. "We put in four other proposals, but it's hard to get someone to take a chance on a startup."

Serious work was needed on the building, including electrical, water lines and all new sewers. Since time is money, Meeker needed to open Mother Bunch before the brewhouse was fully built-out. On opening day, the twenty

Julie Meeker, the engine behind Mother Bunch Brewing. *Courtesy of Julie Meeker.*

taps were filled with all Arizona-brewed beers. Today, thirteen to fifteen handles are Mother Bunch beers, including one nitro handle plus one cask.

While the faces in the brewery may have changed over the years, the consistency remains the same. "When Jerry wanted to re-retire, he transitioned to Erin Deuble, who later transitioned to Omar Zamora. Omar worked with Jerry at North Mountain," said Meeker.

One of Meeker's homebrew recipes, McBride's Irish Red, 5.6% ABV, 25 IBU, made it to the final round at GABF, but did not medal. The beer is an ode to Meeker's husband, Jimmie McBride, who helps out doing handy work in the brewery.

Stay Tru Pilsner is a traditional classic Czech pilsner featuring Hallertau and Saaz hops. Crisp and clean, this pilsner is just 3.3% ABV. Mother IPA, a traditional West Coast–style IPA, is an easy-drinking classic IPA featuring all centennial hops.

The social aspect is what draws many people to the brewing industry and it was no different for Meeker. "I love meeting all the people, it's my favorite part of my job," said Meeker.

North Mountain Brewing Company

Rob Berkner got an early start on his beer education. On a family trip to Europe in 1985, the high school–aged Berkner was allowed to enjoy one beer with each family meal. Partaking in the standard bitters that were common in British pubs at the time, Berkner experienced good beer before understanding the difference. When that trip extended into Belgium, coinciding with the country's equivalent to Oktoberfest, he got to experience beer culture at its finest, along with some of the world's best-made beers.

Continuing his "education" back in the States, Berkner realized there was a difference in quality in the United States compared with what he experienced overseas. Wanting to try to create something more European, he brewed his first batch of beer in 1993. He claims his batch of extract stout was marginally drinkable, but his friends raved about it, giving him the encouragement to brew again.

Homebrewing continued regularly for the better part of the next twenty years. After designing a book of recipes and achieving consistency with his processes, Berkner decided he wanted a change from his day job installing signs. He began to chart his course toward professional brewing.

Enrolling in Chicago's esteemed Siebel Institute of Brewing, Berkner wanted to build on the advanced knowledge he learned on his own. The idea of starting his own brewery was quite a leap of faith, especially at that time. It was 2007, and Berkner was married with three small children. Reinventing himself at that point of his life took guts, determination and patience from his family. Siebel gave him the confidence to move forward and the credibility to approach investors he needed to back his project.

While the brewing industry is notorious for delays, red tape, difficulties with government entities and equipment issues, Berkner's brewery journey was all that and a whole lot more. Acquiring property in the Sunnyslope neighborhood of Phoenix just before Halloween in 2010, he was energized, prepared and ready to build his brewery. Berkner recalled one fateful meeting with Phoenix city government.

"During the design of this building, I got a set of blueprints that had a dotted line that ran straight through the building. I was told the line didn't mean anything and that it didn't apply to me," Berkner said. "The day I went to get final approval to start construction, they told me this dotted line that runs through the property meant that I couldn't build on the other side of the line, effectively cutting my proposed building in half. The person that told me not to worry about it was the same person that delivered the bad news," he said.

After multiple meetings with city hall trying to work out a compromise, the city wouldn't budge. At his wit's end, Berkner called his real estate agent from the steps of the city hall building and told him to put the property back on the market. He was done fighting.

When all seemed lost, Berkner received a call the very next day from the city. They had reconsidered his perspective and decreed he could move forward with his original building plans after all. The project was back on track, at least until the next hurdle appeared. "They did make concessions, but we still had to completely redesign the building," Berkner said.

As the building was being constructed, the walls of the north side of the building were getting somewhat close to a powerline pole behind the building. The power company balked, authorities were contacted and the construction project was immediately halted. Progress stalled for about four months while the two sides worked out an agreement that allowed Berkner to move forward, after footing the bill for relocating the powerlines underground at a substantial, unplanned cost.

Years in and tremendously over budget, Berkner forged ahead. Buoyed by his investors encouraging him to "go big or go home," he put the finishing touches on the brewery. As the opening date neared, he found himself sleeping on a cot in the brewery, trying to grab a nap in between overseeing the completion of the final projects. In March 2013, the doors opened and family and friends were invited in for a soft opening.

They must have had a big family with a lot of friends, because, before he knew it, Berkner's place was at two to three times capacity, filled with people who had been awaiting a taste of the neighborhood's first brewery. After two and a half years of seemingly insurmountable obstacles, he didn't have the heart to turn anyone away. A party for the ages ensued.

When Berkner appeared in front of the packed house, he was given a standing ovation, making every delay, disappointment and heartache melt away in one amazing, emotion-filled moment. On March 15, 2013, North Mountain Brewing Company officially opened for business to the public, instantly becoming an iconic part of Phoenix's Sunnyslope neighborhood.

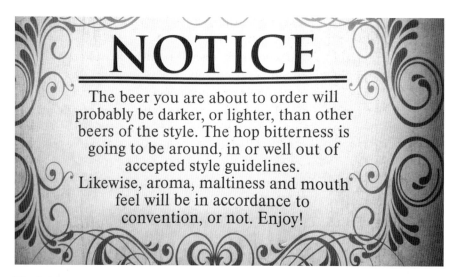

NOTICE

The beer you are about to order will probably be darker, or lighter, than other beers of the style. The hop bitterness is going to be around, in or well out of accepted style guidelines. Likewise, aroma, maltiness and mouth feel will be in accordance to convention, or not. Enjoy!

The lighthearted attitude of North Mountain Brewing.

A full brewpub, North Mountain offers a complete menu and at least a dozen high-quality house beers. The burgers are some of the best in the city, and the beer styles are wonderfully diverse.

Whether it was the challenges he faced getting the brewery open or the day he inadvertently nicked a valve lock that resulted in instantaneously losing a full batch of freshly brewed porter, Berkner is a man who seems to be able to take things in stride. He's tough, just like his neighborhood.

Sunnyslope is a tight-knit community where local businesses support one another. Slope Records, an iconic neighborhood punk record label founded by Tom Lopez, resides there. With a shared affinity for music, Berkner and Lopez connected and collaborated on a beer series called Dead Hero. The series is intended to be a tribute to departed rock stars. Rest in Porter, the first in the series, was released in late 2018.

Some of North Mountain's beers are made specifically to traditional style guidelines, while others are Berkner's reimagination of styles with his own personal twists. Inside jokes and subtle musical themes appear in the beer names.

Grooving With The Pict Scottish Ale, 6.3% ABV, 21 IBU, a reference to an obscure Pink Floyd song, is a traditional Scottish ale. One of the finest examples of the style made stateside, Pict is crafted true to the authentic versions of Scotland featuring rich malt with a hint of smoke on the front of the palate that fades quickly into a clean, dry finish.

THIS BEER IS CHOCOLATY, NUTTY, AND CRISPY. IT IS TASTY!

HAPPY SEED

HEMP ALE

(THIS BEER WILL MAKE YOU SO HAPPY!)

522 E. DUNLAP AVE PHOENIX AZ 85020 WWW.NORTHMOUNTAINBREWING.COM

Happy Seed—Phoenix's first beer made with hemp seeds.

Happy Seed Hemp Ale., 4.5% ABV, 20 IBU, is a tasty brown ale made with Canadian hemp seeds. The first beer produced with hemp in the state of Arizona, the hemp produces complex sunflower flavors that complement the nutty flavors of the malt.

The 5.9% ABV, 16 IBU C.R.E.E.M. Golden Ale is brewed with oats, rye and Arizona wildflower honey, giving extra flavor to this easy-drinking ale. Often mistaken for a cream ale, C.R.E.E.M. is an acronym representing the names of the five people in Berkner's family: Candy, Rob, Emmilie, Erin and Megan.

N.I.B. Imperial Stout is an ode to Black Sabbath, which has a classic song of the same name, as big and dark as this huge 13.2% ABV, 64 IBU imperial stout.

All the brewers who have ever worked at the brewery were invited back to collaborate on a winter beer, released on the 2018 winter solstice, named Ghost of Brewers Past. Each was required to contribute one ingredient that represented something special. With a diverse background of brewers came a wide-ranging assortment of ingredients that included cinnamon, ginger, maple syrup, pinecones, puerquitos (a molasses Mexican sweet bread) and even hard Christmas candy.

Speaking of candy, Berkner's wife, Candy, has been by his side throughout the entire process. Handling marketing, human resources, sales and brewpub operations, she played a huge role in creating the North Mountain brand. Rob handles the head brewing duties, assisted by brewers Greg O'Donohue and Miguel Hidalgo.

In six short years, North Mountain Brewing Company has become an iconic destination, bringing together lovers of great beer far and wide. With a great kitchen, a wide variety of quality-brewed beer styles and a friendly and knowledgeable staff, the Berkners have created a destination place that ranks among Phoenix's finest.

Phoenix Ale Brewery

The Phoenix rose by way of the Emerald City where George Hancock got his start in the beer world. George and his partners bought small Hart Brewing of Kalama, Washington, in the late 1980s. Producing two to three thousand barrels per year, Hart didn't appear destined to become a rising star in the growing craft beer world. One of the beer brands in the brewery's portfolio was called Pyramid, a name the partners liked.

Renaming the company after that beer, Hancock had big plans for Pyramid Brewing, including wanting a big-city address. Purchasing land near the high-traffic area of the Kingdome in Seattle, Washington, provided ample opportunity for growth while positioning the brand in a bustling metropolis.

Still called "microbrew," this new beer movement was gaining popularity. With an energized group ready to leverage the brewery's new name and location, Pyramid was poised for success. In a few short years, Pyramid grew to become a national force and eventually went public through an IPO.

Hancock was the CEO and a member of the board of directors from 1995 to 2008. During that time, the company strategically grew market by market. Selling beers across the country, Pyramid produced upward of 200,000 barrels of beer per year. The brewery excelled in the Southwest, where area sales manager Greg Fretz, known as "Fretzy," was doing a fantastic job placing Pyramid everywhere he could.

After many years of consistent growth, the company was acquired by North American Breweries of Rochester, New York. Upon completion of the sale, Hancock was free to pursue other interests.

Taking the next two years off, he considered other opportunities. Meanwhile, Fretz continued to pound the pavement all over the southwestern United States, now selling beer for Deschutes Brewery.

Based in Phoenix, Fretz kept in touch with his friend and former boss Hancock, discussing the opportunity Phoenix possessed for a well-positioned brewery. Hancock was not immediately convinced, but neither did he rule it out.

Eventually, the two sat down and talked at length, including discussing logistics for opening a brewery. Around 2010, a plan started taking shape that included seeking a large low-rent warehouse facility able to house a production brewery. They leased space at 30th Street and McDowell in Phoenix. Originally, the plan was to make beer for distribution only, with no taproom. The partners worked diligently, and Phoenix Ale Brewery opened in June 2011.

Phoenix Ale Brewery had no connection with the former Phoenix Brewing Company, producers of the highly popular A-1 brand. The name was simply an ode to the city in which they were located with "ale" a precursor to the mostly English-style beers the brewery planned to craft.

Changing course about six months after opening, they created a mobile taproom by rolling portable kegerators across the brewery to the loading dock door and sliding the giant doors open. Operating a few days per week, the makeshift taproom was met with local area support.

The ability to interact with customers created a personal connection with the brewery, creating loyal followers of Phoenix Ale. Realizing the taproom was more important than they originally realized, Hancock and Fretz decided to build a dedicated space. An unused storage area was converted to a full-fledged taproom and retail store that opened in early 2012.

The initial year-round offerings were Camelback IPA, Fretzy's Unfiltered Pale Ale and Watermelon Ale. Fretzy's Pale Ale took off out of the gate, becoming the brewery's no. 1 seller, no surprise since the beer was named after the lead salesperson, Fretz.

Later came Ironwood Porter, WheatStalk Imperial Hefeweizen, Biltmore Blonde and the Keeper Bier de Garde. As the industry changed, so did the styles. As IPAs became the most popular craft beer style nationwide, Camelback IPA became the brewery's top seller.

Current head brewer Nick Hancock, son of George, has a personal favorite in Camelback IPA, an English-style IPA. The combination of English East Kent Goldings and American Cascade hops produces the beer's unique flavor and aroma profile.

Biltmore Blonde is a light-drinking golden ale designed for the heat of the valley. It's a perfect gateway beer for someone trying to move from macro-produced beer to craft.

The popularity of Camelback IPA spawned the brewery's no. 3 seller, Orange Peel IPA. Additions of orange peel and Chinook hops release beautiful aromas, differentiating the brew from its base beer, Camelback IPA.

George Hancock had a simple vision for what he wanted Phoenix Ale Brewery to be. The brewery's mission was to brew delicious, quaffable beers. Hancock had no interest in creating "wow" factor by making unusual beers for beer geeks. He wanted to create a brewery Phoenix residents would be proud to call their own.

On one given afternoon, Hancock took note of the wide variety of clientele in the taproom. White- and blue-collar workers enjoyed beers side by side, from mechanics and landscapers to lawyers and salespeople. Phoenix Ale Brewery's taproom wasn't the place to be or be seen; it was simply a place to go to enjoy good beer. Hancock's vision was coming to pass.

Richard Stark was the CEO of NYPD Pizza, a local chain of New York–style pizza restaurants. In 2012, Stark was well aware of craft beer's rising popularity and was keenly aware of the way people regularly supported local brands. Since beer was the top-selling beverage sold at the pizza chain, Stark wanted to explore the possibility of partnering with a local brewery to make a "house" beer that paired well with NYPD's top-selling meat-topped pies.

A good friend of Stark's was the CEO of Republic Distributing, now called Young's Market Company. The friend suggested he reach out to Greg Fretz to gauge the brewery's interest in producing the pizza chain's house beer. Fretz and Hancock both loved the idea. The three men sat down to work out details.

As they conversed, Hancock explained his company's mission and the vision of its beers with Stark. Stark then met with John Donehower, Phoenix Ale Brewery's first brewmaster. The group agreed an amber ale seemed most appropriate to pair with the meat-topped pizzas. Donehower suggested picking up an assortment of ambers on the market, ranging from malty to hoppy, to do proper research.

The next step was to schedule a tasting, pairing the various ambers with six different pizzas. According to Stark, Donehower did a thorough job of putting together a questionnaire geared toward the flavor attributes of the beers and pizzas. Each of the fifteen participants had to try each beer with each pizza and then rate them. Donehower tabulated the results and put together a preferred flavor profile. From the information gathered, he made a test batch.

About four weeks later, another group of fifteen was brought in and the process was repeated, now with the test beer in the mix. Donehower processed that information, then brewed a second test batch.

Finally, a larger group of about forty people was assembled in one of the restaurants to replicate the true consumer experience. This tasting took place in November 2012, with Donehower hosting yet another survey. Several menu items were served in addition to the pizzas to gauge the beer's appeal with other dishes. The results showed a 97 percent approval rating. About three weeks later, the beer was available and ready to be served. It was named NYPD Uptown Amber Ale.

Restaurant staff members embraced and promoted the beer heavily. Pint glasses were designed with both the Uptown Amber and Phoenix Ale Brewery's logos. It was the only beer served in these special glasses. NYPD Pizza promoted the fact that this beer was available only within the confines of its restaurants. In a very short time, Uptown Amber Ale became NYPD Pizza's best-selling beer.

Phoenix Ale Brewery's growth continued when it had the good fortune of placing its beers inside Chase Field, home of the Arizona Diamondbacks. Exposure in a venue of that size can be a game changer, and it definitely put Phoenix Ale Brewery on the map.

Besides producing its own beers, Phoenix Ale Brewery began brewing the portfolio of Sonoran Brewing Company in 2013, including its popular White Chocolate. The company brewed Sonoran's beers for the next five years.

In May 2013, tragedy struck Phoenix Ale Brewery when Greg Fretz became ill and passed away at the age of forty-seven. Fretz had been Hancock's right-hand man since their days together at Pyramid, and he was the main reason Hancock took the leap of faith to relocate to Arizona and open a brewery. Fretz's death was a huge blow to everyone at Phoenix Ale Brewery, especially Hancock.

It was also a blow to Stark, who had become good friends with Fretz during the creation of Uptown Amber. With Fretz's passing, Stark's relationship grew closer with the elder Hancock. In spring 2014, the two had lunch, and Stark proposed the idea of doing a Phoenix Ale/NYPD joint brewpub. Stark was intrigued by the idea of having a nanobrewery inside of a restaurant.

That idea never came to pass once Stark began to consider new opportunities outside the NYPD Pizza franchise. He and his financial partners agreed to part ways, and by December 2014, Stark was no longer affiliated with NYPD Pizza.

Stark noticed that when he'd visit local brewpubs, the quality of the food usually did not match that of the beer. As craft beer was gaining popularity, people were becoming more sophisticated. Craft was finally getting into restaurants. Stark saw a gap in the local market. He felt he could raise the bar with great beer and food in an environment that supported both. He envisioned a community ale house, a neighborhood go-to place for families, complete with a dog-friendly patio that appealed to beer and non-beer drinkers alike.

Reaching back out to Hancock, the two put together a strategic relationship in early 2015. Stark conceptualized a gastropub celebrating craft food and beers with a menu utilizing Phoenix Ale's beers both as pairings and as ingredients within the various entrées. The staff would be extensively trained by brewery personnel to become beer savvy and to fully understand the brewery's story. The restaurant would be filled with brewery décor, bringing elements of the brew house into the restaurant.

Stark successfully raised money from April to June 2015, then signed a letter of intent for a location on 7th Street in Phoenix. The property suited Stark's vision of an urban ale house. Construction began on January 1, 2016, and Phoenix Ale Brewery Central Kitchen opened for business on May 11, 2016.

As Central Kitchen is a family-friendly establishment that emphasizes both the beer and the food, the menu was designed to appeal to people of all shapes, sizes, ages and lifestyles. Popular menu items include the house-made pretzel bites made with the King George Amber, served with Biltmore Blonde cheese fondue and Ironwood Porter mustard; Biltmore Blonde–battered Alaskan cod and chips; and the brewmaster black iron pizza made with King George Amber dough topped with house sauce, smoked mozzarella, pepperoni, sausage and bacon.

Of the sixteen beers on tap, seven are Phoenix Ale Brewery beers. The one with the most interesting story may be King George Amber Ale. According to Stark, "We intended to offer the Uptown Amber as part of the Phoenix Ale Brewery Central Kitchen's beer offerings. Naturally, we weren't

The bar at Phoenix Ale Brewery & Central Kitchen. *Courtesy of PAB.*

Action abounds at Phoenix Ale Brewery & Central Kitchen. *Courtesy of PAB.*

interested in calling it Uptown Amber. Through our advertising agency, we decided to do a naming contest on social media in March."

"Sadly, George's health was declining quickly and he passed away in mid-March. Still four to six weeks away from opening the restaurant, we knew the beer needed to be named in George's honor. Our top two finalists were Sir George Amber Ale and King George Amber Ale. George's son Nick felt 'King George' seemed the most fitting. The emotional attachment to this beer came from co-creating it with Greg, George and John Donehower; from the origin of the beer and the collaboration, to the genesis for this idea of the Central Kitchen concept."

George Hancock and Greg Fretz were beer industry veterans who created a Phoenix brewery that made beer for the people of Phoenix. Though Hancock and Fretz are no longer here, their legacies continue. George's son Nick Hancock heads the brewing operations at Phoenix Ale Brewery, which he and his family now own. Richard Stark keeps the spirit of George and Greg alive with his community ale house pairing great food with the fine beers of the Phoenix Ale Brewery.

Sun Up/Sonoran Brewing

A shining star of the Phoenix area brewing scene for over two decades, Sun Up's story is about change and evolution. One constant in the Sun Up story is the man behind the beer, German-born brewmaster Uwe Boer. Born in the old-world German brewing town of Dortmund in 1960, Boer masterfully crafts IPAs and stouts with the same precision as the lagers of his home country.

Boer came to the United States in 1981, landing in San Diego, California. He spent fifteen years there learning the nuances of the American way of life, including its beers. Taking up the art of homebrewing, he started brewing beer from a mail-order kit, upgrading to extract batches before taking the plunge into all-grain brewing.

Boer and a friend named Paul Gunn honed their homebrewing skills for about three years. Gunn relocated to Phoenix and opened a homebrew supply store known as GunnBrew. Before he left, Gunn encouraged Boer to consider taking his hobby professional, believing he was a natural. Working an unsatisfying warehouse job at the time, Boer heeded Gunn's advice, honing his skills further.

Meanwhile, in Phoenix, a man named John Watt was planning to open a new brewery. Located in an urban village called Maryvale on Phoenix's west side, the Portland, Oregon transplant Watt saw opportunity in the growing southwestern desert market. Calling his new brewery Sonora Brewing Company, Watt worked with an architect named John Westberg, who helped get required documents through the City of Phoenix. As the brewery neared completion, all Watt needed was a full-time brewer to run the brewing operations. Enter Uwe Boer.

Opening around the same time as another new start-up brewery named Four Peaks, Sonora Brewing, located at 36th Avenue and Indian School Road, developed a following with beers including Sonora Desert Amber Ale, Westside Wheat, Old Saguaro Barleywine and Inebriator Imperial Stout.

In 2001, a former salesman of the brewery named Norm Horn took on an important new role. Horn opened an English-style pub named Sonora Brewhouse Pub, exclusively pouring Sonora Brewing Company beers. He hired John Westberg to repurpose an old house into his pub concept—the same Westberg who helped Watt get Sonora Brewing open years earlier. The pub opened in the heart of Central Phoenix on Camelback Road.

Sonora Brewing Company (Watt) and Sonora Brewhouse Pub (Horn) coexisted as independently owned entities. The marketplace often confused

Uwe Boer, legendary brewmaster, Sun Up Brewing.

Sonora Brewing Company for a Mexican brewery. Watt added the *n* to "Sonora," hoping to lessen confusion. Sonoran Brewing Company began a successful distribution campaign, placing its beer in twenty-six Trader Joe's stores in California.

Despite having Horn's pub exclusively selling its beers, the brewery's sales plateaued around two thousand barrels. Feeling that the brewery had reached its peak, Watt shifted his focus from brewery owner to brewing tank manufacturer. In 2004, Watt sold Sonoran's equipment, moved back to Portland, Oregon, and started Stout Brewing Systems, a company Watt successfully operates to this day.

Upon the closing of the brewery, Sonora Brewhouse Pub expanded into the adjacent building, adding brewing equipment. This gave Sonora the ability to produce its own beer. Horn hired Boer to brew the house beers.

Meanwhile, Boer's former assistant brewer was a young, entrepreneurial type named Scott Yarosh. He had a vision of creating his own brewery but had neither a line of beers nor a brewery of his own in which to brew them. Capitalizing on an opportunity, Yarosh acquired the name and distribution rights to brew Sonoran Brewing Company beers.

With a brewery name and distribution rights in hand, Yarosh struck gold when he connected with the owners of the former Pinnacle Peak Brewing Company in Scottsdale. Pinnacle Peak had shuttered its brewery, now operating solely as a restaurant. The owners were happy to have Yarosh reemploy the dormant equipment, and Yarosh effectively created a new brewing company out of thin air.

The agreement dictated Yarosh could distribute beers in the marketplace and Boer could brew beers exclusively for the pub. The two brewers coexisted, brewing similarly named beers for about five years. For a period of time, Yarosh contract brewed beers for Papago Brewing Company in addition to brewing Sonoran beers.

In 2005, Boer brought back an old recipe from the early days called Inebriator Imperial Stout. Tweaking the original recipe, Boer replaced his "dry hop" regimen with an addition of coffee. The change reduced the hop character while introducing a flavorful coffee essence to complement the chocolate and roast flavors of the base beer.

The full-bodied black ale drank with a rich, creamy mouthfeel. Boer renamed the beer White Russian Imperial Stout. The beer gained instant popularity and developed an almost cult-like following, becoming the brewery's second best-selling beer behind the flagship Trooper IPA.

In 2009, Sonora Brewhouse Pub was approached by local distributor Crescent Crown about distributing Trooper IPA. The contract with Yarosh wouldn't allow Boer to distribute unless Sonora changed its name. Seeing opportunity for growth through distribution, Horn renamed his company Sun Up Brewing.

A loyal audience began to rally around Boer's beers. Leading the way was Trooper IPA, checking in at 6.2% ABV and 60 IBU. Hop varietals Simcoe, Columbus and Falconer's Flight created a perfect hoppy blend. Trooper remains the no. 1 seller in the Sun Up brewpub.

White Russian took off like a rocket, captivating beer aficionados and casual beer drinkers alike, featured regularly in area "best of" lists. Hitting the market through distribution in 2015, White Russian has become the brewery's signature beer and no. 1 seller outside the brewpub, despite being a 9.4% ABV monster of a beer.

As Norm Horn neared retirement, he was looking for a buyer for his business. John and Sindi Westberg appeared on the scene one more time, purchasing the brewpub and adjacent properties. The additional space provided Sun Up with the ability to expand operations and increase production.

As of summer 2018, Sun Up annually produces about 1,500 barrels of beer, much of which is consumed in its popular brewpub. According to Boer, distribution is expected to grow with strategic placements in popular retail locations throughout Arizona.

Sun Up's White Russian Imperial Stout.

Through the years, Boer regularly contract brewed beers for other breweries. At one time, he (like Yarosh) contract brewed beers for Papago Brewing Company and currently produces beers for the popular Scottsdale's Craft 64 and the nascent Four Silos Brewing and Coffee Company.

Boer created a barrel-aging program, adding a whole new dimension to the Sun Up lineup. Using wine, bourbon and tequila barrels, Boer marries the flavors in the barrels with those of his finely crafted beers to produce new masterpieces. One of those is a braggot (mead) named Sunna's Nektar that is barrel aged eighteen months—750ml bottles sold for seventy-five dollars per bottle.

Uwe Boer has been a fixture in the Arizona brewing scene for over two decades. Popular and well-respected, Boer eagerly shares his knowledge of beer and brewing with aspiring brewers, many of whom have gone on to professional careers of their own. "It has been a lot of fun to teach and see others grow," said Uwe. "It's like raising kids."

No matter how many styles Boer has brewed over the years, the man who grew up in Dortmund, Germany, still loves to brew, and enjoy, a classic German pilsner. He is very proud of the authentically crafted pilsner he makes, knowing it is one of the most difficult beer styles to brew. Whether it's the pilsner, White Russian or otherwise, it only takes a few sips of any of Sun Up's beers to cement Uwe Boer's legacy as one of Phoenix's finest brewmasters.

The company of many names started by John Watt and reimagined by Norm Horn remains a Phoenix brewing landmark, under the watchful eye of current owners John and Sindi Westberg. Sun Up Brewing is as popular as ever and continues to develop new beers to complement the traditional favorites. The beers of Sonoran Brewing Company also continue to be part of the local beer scene, being contract brewed by various breweries.

Wren House Brewing Company

Wanting to pay homage to their beloved state of Arizona, the partners behind Wren House Brewing Company wanted to incorporate the state bird, the cactus wren, into the brewery name. Those partners include Drew Pool, a Phoenix native who handles all aspects of marketing, including the branding, sales, customer service and media. Bill Hammond, a tech industry veteran, handles the business side of the brewery as well as tackling research and development. University of Montana graduate Preston Thoeny is the head brewer, handling all brewery operations.

Hammond and Pool were the first to the party. According to Pool, "Scouring the earth for the best ingredients to make an awesome product is the true essence of being in craft, and what drew us to the industry. Bill and I came together over a chance meeting at a charity event. We talked about building a company, and we rallied around the beer business because of our mutual interest and the opportunities in that field."

Thoeny's introduction into the fold was equal parts good connections and great timing. "Bill and Drew began looking for a brewer, and Drew's wife and I had grown up together," said Thoeny. "They reached out while I was in Montana and asked if I had any Arizona recommendations. My wife and I were interested in moving back home, so it worked out perfectly," he said.

Thoeny was introduced to craft beer during his college days. Missoula had many high-quality craft breweries that helped him quickly develop his palate. Passion for beer turned into a quest to brew it, which he pursued with a laser focus.

The partners divided and conquered to bring this small Phoenix brewery into existence. Unlike many of their industry counterparts, they didn't encounter many long delays or government-related hurdles. Working as a team, they forged a solid camaraderie as they built the brewery.

Located in Phoenix's Green Gables neighborhood, the property that houses Wren House sat unoccupied for decades. Falling in love with the building's character, the partners rebuilt the old guest house and garage into the brewhouse and converted the main 1920s bungalow house into a cozy taproom.

Left to right: Bill, Preston and Drew of Wren House Brewing. *Courtesy of Wren House.*

When the brewery opened in June 2015, locals and beer aficionados flocked to experience the new brewery on the block. People took notice, and word spread quickly. Focusing on quality while exploring a wide range of brewing techniques and styles, Thoeny integrates international beer styles and cutting-edge craft creations that satiate and stimulate the senses.

The Wally series of beers are triple IPAs that utilize a variety of hops from all over the world. Good Boy Wally kicked off the series. Big Spill Pils, Thoeny's personal favorite, is a light, flavorful pilsner that is dry hopped with non-traditional Nelson Sauvin hops. The dry-hopping addition provides a white wine note that sets it apart from other lagers.

Checking in at over 10% ABV, Kingsnake is a barrel-aged stout aged on a bed of the finest vanilla beans, resulting in a thick, roasty, chocolate/vanilla dessert beer. Kolsch is made in the traditional German essence, with just a hint of honey malt added for extra flavor.

Wren House packages beers in sixteen-ounce cans via mobile canning. Most are sold in the taproom, though some are self-distributed along with kegs, making Wren House beer available throughout Arizona.

The passion and focus on their customers are evident in everything Wren House does. "All of our successes come from our customers, who help inspire us and continue to be passionate about what we do," said Thoeny.

EAST VALLEY BREWERIES

Arizona Wilderness

Movie sets, calendars and car commercials have showcased the beauty of the Arizona wilderness for years. Now residents and visitors alike can enjoy a taste of the Arizona Wilderness in a glass.

Voted best new brewery by RateBeer.com in 2014, Arizona Wilderness came on the scene faster than the spread of a desert wildfire. It was founded by a native Arizonan and an Ohio transplant who may look like brothers, but their only relation is their shared vision for making great beer in homage to all things Arizona.

When they are not hiking, camping or doing another beer collaboration somewhere in the world, owners Jonathan Buford and Patrick Ware are dreaming up innovative ways to reimagine beer. Believing anything is possible is the driving force behind the successes of this thriving Gilbert brewery.

Jonathan Buford and Patrick Ware (*right*) at the Firestone Walker Invitational.

A native of Arizona, Patrick Ware developed a love for the outdoors, regularly camping and hiking with his dad. During his college days at Arizona State University, he spent equal time studying and brewing. Interning at local brewery Gordon Biersch, Ware learned from Dieter Foerstner, who elevated his homebrewing skills into the professional realm.

Jonathan Buford had lived in several states, most recently leaving Ohio for the opportunities of the Copper State. Traveling across the country in his old Chevy Nova with only a couple hundred dollars to his name, Buford's resourcefulness convinced him he'd succeed wherever he'd land. Finding employment at the Biltmore resort helped him hone his service industry skills. An entrepreneur at heart, he opened and operated a window cleaning company successfully for six years.

Buford enjoyed craft beers and was inspired by the craft beer industry. With visions of eventually opening his own brewery, he absorbed knowledge through audiobooks and podcasts as he washed windows.

He'd frequent local watering holes, where he'd often be confused for someone named Pat. He eventually came to find the mysterious "Pat" was none other than Ware—the two having similar physical characteristics.

By this time, Ware was brewing at SanTan Brewing Company of Chandler. When the two met, Buford shared his vision of opening a brewery that would brew artisan-style craft ales based around an Arizona-based nature theme. Intrigued and inspired, Ware agreed, in principle, to become Buford's head brewer.

Right: Patrick Ware, Arizona Wilderness.

Below: Patrick Ware (*left*) and Jonathan Buford of Arizona Wilderness taking themselves seriously.

When some investment dollars fell through late in the process, Ware's role in the project changed. With less money available to properly pay Ware, Buford offered an ownership stake if Ware would take the plunge and join his fledgling company. Ware and Buford were now partners.

Located in a modest building in suburban Gilbert, Arizona Wilderness Brewing Company opened in September 2013 with a total of seventeen employees. Just six months into its existence, Arizona Wilderness was voted the 2014 Best New Brewery in the World by RateBeer.com, a community of beer enthusiasts dedicated to the pursuit and appreciation of good beer.

Due to the publicity boost from winning the award, the brewery's fortunes changed overnight. Local news stations appeared, requesting interviews. People flocked to the new brewpub, making two-hour waits the norm. The staff doubled, then tripled, to accommodate the crowds. Brewing ramped up considerably, with the brewhouse scrambling to keep up with demand.

With Arizona Wilderness being more a rallying cry than a name, Buford and Ware go to the extreme to incorporate a little taste of Arizona in every glass of their beer. Avid hikers and campers, the pair often spend days in the great outdoors seeking indigenous ingredients to incorporate into their recipes. Anything from mesquite pods to juniper berries have been employed. Buford, a skilled photographer, captures exquisite snapshots during these adventures that are displayed on screens inside the restaurant.

On one occasion, they took this concept to the extreme, inviting notable brewers to participate in a weekend of beer making in the desert, employing the naturally occurring microflora of Arizona.

Buford, Ware and head brewer Chase Saraiva invited more than twenty of the world's most innovative brewers to participate. Brewers from Tired Hands, Creature Comforts, Almanac, Firestone Walker, Other Half, Jackie O's, Jester King and others spent the weekend together creating this nature-kissed work of art. More than just a brewing experience, the group built a camaraderie as they shared brewing knowledge.

The project started by brewing wort (the precursor to beer) in the brewery, then transporting it three hours north to the Arizona high country, where they let the naturally occurring microflora of Arizona's wilderness inoculate the beer.

Using open vessels known as coolships, the beer was exposed to the elements, allowing any naturally occurring fermentable microorganisms to enter the cooled wort, starting fermentation. Despite this nontraditional brewing technique providing no guarantee of success, Buford and Ware

Chase Saraiva, head brewer, Arizona Wilderness.

persevered. The willingness to take these types of risks to see ideas become reality is what sets Arizona Wilderness Brewing apart from its competition.

In another example of showcasing the Arizona Wilderness in a glass, the team created Connection Saison, a Belgian-style beer made predominantly from ingredients grown within the state of Arizona.

Working together with Hauser & Hauser Farms and the Nature Conservancy, the brewers created a beer made from locally grown hops and barley. This particular strain of barley provided multiple benefits. Besides providing Arizona breweries with fresh, local barley, it also helped reduce the amount of water farmers drew from the Verde River to water crops.

Hauser & Hauser Farms agreed to replace some alfalfa and corn crops with the barley. Barley requires far less water than does alfalfa. And while barley and corn use similar amounts of water, barley needs it most in the spring when the river is relatively high. Corn relies on water in the heart of the summer, straining the river's water supply. Not only did the grain make a positive environmental impact, it also helped produce a fantastic tasting beer.

Anything but creatures of habit, Arizona Wilderness brewers take pride in continually reinterpreting and creating new beer styles. It's rare to visit the brewpub and regularly see the same beers on tap. A rare mainstay is Refuge IPA, the 6.8% ABV flagship offering that has been a crowd favorite since day one. A beer that has evolved over the years, Refuge IPA packs a hoppy

Arizona Wilderness, a name and a way of life.

punch of flavor and aromatics reminiscent of pine and citrus with just the right amount of bitterness.

Another crowd favorite, when available, is the fall seasonal Picacho Pecan Pie Brown Ale. A Northern English brown ale inspired by pecan pie, this beer checks in at 8% ABV and is brewed with vanilla beans, maple syrup and Arizona-sourced pecans and lactose.

Superstition Coffee Stout is a coffee and stout lover's dream, made with local coffee from Superstition Coffee Company, along with roasted malts and oatmeal. Tongan vanilla beans add a touch of sweetness to create the perfect balance to this 6.5% black ale.

Everything about the brewery centers on Arizona, including building relationships with local farmers and businesses. Sourcing local is always a priority, including trading spent grain to farmers who provide beef for the brewpub's extensive menu.

Continued success allowed Arizona Wilderness to expand onsite, opening an additional tasting room. Within this room resided Ware's baby: a humidity-controlled barrel-aging and sour room to satisfy the pair's fondness for Belgian-inspired brewing.

That was just the beginning of the expansion. A new beer garden location opened in February 2019 in downtown Phoenix, bringing their brand of Arizona-inspired craft food and beers to the epicenter of the Southwest. Additionally, they opened an offsite warehouse to serve as the new aging facility for their Belgian and sour beers while the space that previously served that purpose has become a conditioning room for lagers and beers that require extended aging.

Well respected in the worldwide brewing community, Buford and Ware utilize their relationships to collaborate with other brewers as often as possible. The list of collaborations is extensive, but some of the notable collaborations have taken place with Brasserie du Brabant, Scratch, Stillwater, Modern Times, Jolly Pumpkin and London's Beavertown Brewery, a brewery owned by Logan Plant, the son of Led Zeppelin vocalist Robert Plant.

Arizona Wilderness has brought to life what Buford and Ware's minds envisioned. Wanting to create a community-centered meeting place that brought together innovative artisan ales, high-quality, locally sourced food and an appreciation for the Arizona landscape, they have exceeded even their own wildest dreams in creating one of Arizona's most innovative and exciting breweries.

Beer Research Institute Story

Part alchemy and part passion, the Beer Research Institute was founded by Matt Trethewey and Greg Sorrels, longtime friends who met in 1999 and share a common love for all things craft beer. Growing up in Northern California's Humboldt County, Greg was introduced to several small breweries in his community, including Mad River Brewing, which played an important role in developing his palate for craft beer.

Likewise, Matt visited his first brewpub, local Tempe powerhouse Four Peaks, and was wowed by how much flavor was crammed into each beer. While Four Peaks may have planted the seed, Matt's official indoctrination into the craft beer world happened when he experienced the beers of New Belgium Brewery of Fort Collins, Colorado. It was an "aha" moment for Matt, who immediately began his quest for better quality beer.

Matt became intrigued with the notion of making his own beer. In the fall of 2005, he went to a local homebrew supply store and bought his first kit. Matt recalled the batch of beer that made him catch the brewing bug. "I brewed the beer, fumbling the whole time, but at the end of the day I made beer. It turned out horrible, but I drank every drop of it because I made it myself and I was still proud of it. It was a pale ale that wound up having a very astringent hop profile. That didn't matter; I was hooked."

Greg Sorrels (*left*) and Matt Trewelany of BRI. *Courtesy of BRI.*

Matt brewed regularly, anytime the opportunity presented itself. Eventually, Greg volunteered to help Matt brew a batch. "Greg came over for that brew and was hooked. Every batch we've made after that day has been made together. We brewed about 225 batches of homebrew before BRI opened, using the last year to fine tune recipes, processes and our system," recalled Matt.

During that run, the two friends delved deep into their beer research. They read every beer-brewing book they could find. They joined online brewing groups and message boards. The two listened to many podcasts on brewing and even joined the local homebrew club.

The research started to pay dividends. The beer improved, and the friends entered competitions. In the very first one they entered, they won a couple of bronze medals, validating their improving work. The two continued to refine their processes and recipes and then entered the same beers into other competitions. The bronze medals turned into golds.

Around that time, Matt and Greg started toying with the idea of possibly taking their hobby to the professional level. They both had business backgrounds, Matt in the restaurant industry and Greg in the contracting world. One day, Matt dropped the bomb. "I said, I'm going to cash out of my company and open a brewery. Do you want in on that? Thankfully, he said yes."

Matt took the plunge in the fall of 2013, leaving his former company and starting the planning process for BRI. It took just over a year from conception of the idea to opening the doors. The Beer Research Institute opened for business on November 17, 2014, in a strip mall in Mesa, Arizona.

"The name is more of a goof than anything. It makes us sound super official, but really, we're just a couple of jackasses making big beers! It's a conversation starter. Some people ask if we're a school or a homebrew shop and we get to tell our story. When branding the brewery, we didn't want to be the standard 'XYZ Brewing Co.' or 'XYZ Aleworks' so we were trying to come up with something different," said Matt.

"It was sort of an ongoing, inside joke. I'd be at a brewery drinking a beer and I'd take a picture of the beer and the menu board and send it to Greg, saying 'I'm conducting more research.' That started going back and forth between the two of us for a while. When we were ready to brand our brewery, I asked what he thought of the name 'Beer Research Institute.' We both thought it was solid, and I filed the legal paperwork the very next day," Matt added.

While the two brew every batch of beer together, they divide up the company's responsibilities according to each other's strengths. Greg is responsible for the overall brewing operation, and Matt handles company leadership and marketing.

The company lives by a straightforward and simple mantra. According to Matt, "BRI focuses on the beers we want to drink and the food we want to eat. It's a labor of love and passion. That's the way it's been since the garage days, and it's the way it is now."

As its name would suggest, BRI likes to get experimental. However, there are a few regular "house" beers that loyal customers have come to crave. The 480G IPA is the flagship offering. Checking in at 8% ABV and 71 IBU, 480G is a traditional West Coast IPA showcasing Simcoe and Amarillo hops. Besides being the brewery's best seller, it is also Matt's personal favorite in the lineup.

Lolli Imperial Belgian Blonde is a Belgian-style ale. Lolli clocks in at 8.2% ABV and showcases the nuances of the Belgian yeast strain by producing huge esters of clove, banana and bubblegum. While the hops may be the star of the show with 480G, the yeast takes center stage in Lolli, BRI's no. 2 beer.

The conversation-starting Morning Sex Coffee Sweet Stout is brewed in collaboration with Peixoto Coffee of Chandler. Brewed in the traditional style of a milk stout, a substantial addition of cold brew coffee is added to the batch before the beer is carbonated. The end result is an easy-drinking stout with a huge coffee kick.

Cheers! *Courtesy of BRI.*

According to Matt, "Our adventure in this industry has been amazing and eye opening. It's a tough business that requires constant hustle. We work with some of the best people we've ever known. The industry is very close knit because we're in a 'David and Goliath' scenario. It's all of us small, independent guys bonding together to fight 'big beer.' The relationships we've built will be lifelong, and our base of friends has grown tremendously."

The future is bright at BRI, the duo having recently completed an expansion, doubling the size of the pub and increasing brewing output by 400 percent.

"We make amazing beer and have a vibe that is 100 percent unique to the Arizona beer scene. We're currently the sixth highest-rated brewery in the state of Arizona on the Untappd App and have several beers that are at the top of their respective categories. We love what we do, our customers see that and the finished product pulls it all together," said Matt.

BJ's Brewery and the Rise of Doc Osborne

Born in West Covina, California, Derek Osborne took the road less traveled on his way to becoming a professional brewer. He goes by the nickname "Doc," since he was a chiropractor before becoming a brewer. It was during his studies for chiropractic medicine that he accidentally discovered his true passion: his love of beer making.

With plans to be a chiropractor, Osborne attended the Parker College of Chiropractic Medicine in Dallas, Texas. While achieving a doctorate would be hard work for most people, it presented quite the challenge for Osborne, as he is dyslexic. Undeterred, he found he learned best through listening and observing, rather than reading and memorizing.

One day, while walking through lower Greenville Avenue near the Southern Methodist University campus, he stumbled upon a shop that promoted the sale of every kind of salsa and hot sauce. More unobtrusive at the back of the store was a small mill and different types of barley for sale.

While homebrewing was legal, it was not widely practiced at the time, and shops that sold homebrewing supplies often did so without a lot of fanfare. With his interest piqued, Osborne whimsically purchased a beer-making kit to produce a clone of Cooper's Australian Ale. As homebrewers can relate, the kit was equipped with a can of liquid extract (likely aged and past its prime) with a packet of equally aged dry yeast taped to the underside of the can. While he may not have known it at the time, he was about to learn lesson number one in brewing: always use the best, freshest ingredients when making beer. Those contained in that kit, well, not so much.

That same day, he purchased a book on homebrewing, written by the founder of the American Homebrewers Association, Charlie Papazian, titled *The Complete Joy of Homebrewing*. Inspired and motivated, the dyslexic Osborne read the book cover to cover. His newfound passion seemingly overcame his disorder.

In the mid-1990s, after Osborne had contracted the brewing bug and began to hone his skills, an old red brick building near where he lived in Brea, California, announced itself as the site of a future brewery. Intrigued, Osborne stopped by and made contact with Alex Puchner, the brewmaster of the fledgling brewery-to-be.

Practicing with an established chiropractor as he worked toward passing the boards, Osborne was getting real-life experience without the overhead. Working part time allowed him time to continue mastering his hobby of brewing.

Osborne reached out to Puchner and offered his services on a pro-bono basis. The idea of doing something—anything—for a professional brewery inspired him, even if it came without pay, understanding the value the experience would provide. Puchner offered him an unofficial job sweeping the floors. Osborne redefined the phrase "starting at the bottom and working one's way up."

He kept showing up day after day, sometimes working twelve-hour shifts, without compensation. Puchner was impressed with his dedication, willingness to learn and adeptness toward the science of brewing. While the brewery was still being built, it now had its official name. It was to be called BJ's.

BJ's as an entity already existed at the time but did not brew its own beer. This new brewery would change that. When the brewery finally did open, Osborne became the beer runner, transporting beer to the various BJ's taprooms around the region. And finally, he was added to the payroll.

Nothing long-term was promised to Osborne, since he was still studying for the National Boards. The general assumption was that he would stay on until he passed those and then he'd pursue his chiropractic practice.

When Osborne passed the boards in 1997, he sat down with Puchner to discuss his future. He really enjoyed making beer and envisioned himself more as a professional brewer than as a chiropractor. It just so happened that BJ's was expanding into Boulder, Colorado, and Portland, Oregon, and needed someone to brew the beer. Osborne volunteered to become the brewer in Portland.

He opened that brewery on Jantzen Beach, then helped open a second Oregon location before relocating to take over the Boulder, Colorado operation. He spent three years in Boulder from 1998 to 2001. As the company continued to expand, so did the opportunities. When a new location was set to open in a burgeoning new desert town known as Chandler, Arizona, the warmer and drier climate appealed to the native Californian. He accepted the job to lead the new facility and has lived in Chandler ever since.

Evolution continued as the company continued to grow. Regional brewers were added to ensure a consistency in the quality of the beers. Through years of persistence and dedication, Osborne became the regional head brewer for the Southwest. Eventually, Osborne became director of brewing operations when a new CEO was brought in and when the company did away with regional brewers around 2008. Osborne held this title from 2008 throughout the rest of his tenure with BJ's.

BJ's turned out to be the training grounds for many future brewers of Arizona. One of those brewers was Melissa Phillips, who became a brewing assistant at BJ's before later brewing for Arizona's largest brewery, Four Peaks.

Just friends when they worked together at BJs, Osborne and Phillips eventually began to date. After being together about a year, they took a camping trip to the Mogollon Rim outside of Payson, Arizona, where Osborne proposed. She said yes, and fourteen years later, they not only remain happily married but also are the most medaled brewing household in the state of Arizona.

Prior to the big day, they each brewed a batch of beer to serve at the wedding. She produced "Alt Ball and Chain," a German-style altbier, while he produced a German-style lager named "What the Helles He Thinking?" What more would be expected from a couple of brewers?

Another brewer that got his start at BJ's before going on to bigger opportunities was a midwestern transplant named Jeff Huss. He started as an assistant and worked his way up to head brewer. Today, Jeff and his wife, Leah, own Huss Brewing Company, Arizona's third-largest brewery.

Rob Gagnon learned under Osborne at BJ's and now owns Flying Basset Brewery in Gilbert, Arizona. Travis Herman, another Osborne protégé, teamed up with former Tempe beer man J.P. Watts and co-founded Scofflaw Brewing Company, based in Atlanta, Georgia.

A mutual friend introduced Osborne and Tempe restaurateur Julian Wright. Wright asked for a meeting with Osborne to consult with him about starting a brewery. Wright presented an interesting concept for a European brewery/bistro, showing Osborne the layout of the building. Osborne gladly

Derek "Doc" Osborne, award-winning Pedal Haus brewer. *Courtesy of Pedal Haus.*

shared his industry knowledge and made many recommendations about how to properly build a brewery. He approached the consultation from the perspective of how he would approach it if it was his own brewery, even if he was only a consultant on the project.

The two met again about a week later. During that second meeting, Wright mentioned he was in the market for a brewer. Happily entrenched in a secure, stable position with a solid company, Osborne initially declined. Wright was persistent and knew Osborne was the guy he wanted to run his brewing operations. Persistence paid off, and eventually, Osborne took the leap of faith to join Wright and was offered a minority ownership share in the company.

Osborne stayed on at BJ's for about four months to ensure a smooth transition. Once Pedal Haus received its brewing equipment, Osborne began a new brewing chapter as the head of brewing operations for Pedal Haus.

Greg Larsen, a lead brewer at BJ's Chandler, assumed the title of head brewer upon Osborne's departure. Greg was eventually promoted to the same position at the BJ's production facility in Reno. Joe Baldwin, formerly of Uncle Bear's brewery, came on board and took Larsen's place heading the Chandler location. Eventually, Baldwin was also promoted to the Reno facility, allowing BJ's Chandler assistant brewer Dannon Rusch to elevate to the position of head brewer, a title he holds at the time of this writing.

Derek Osborne has carried on his medal-winning ways with Pedal Haus, while BJ's continues to be a fixture in the Phoenix craft beer scene.

Bone Haus Brewing Company

Bone Haus Brewing Company is more than just another brewery. It's a story that unfolds in every piece of artwork found in the ornately decorated taproom. The Day of the Dead theme, inspired by the ancient catacombs of Europe, takes on a southwestern twist with the tales of the Lost Dutchman folklore. Every piece of art tells a story, just as the beers tell tales of places previously traveled by owner Keith Chapman.

The brainchild of brand master Keith Chapman and brewmaster Andy Weiner, two longtime Fountain Hills residents who wanted to establish a brewery in their hometown, Bone Haus Brewing explores bold and adventurous new flavors. Intent on crafting the best beers imaginable, Weiner often creates unique variations on classic beer styles.

Weiner has been homebrewing for more than twenty-five years and worked in management for Microsoft. Traveling the world, Chapman has enjoyed beers in over twenty different countries. These experiences, and his time working at Fender Musical Instruments and NASA, helped him learn a lot about brand and product development.

As Chapman strives to provide a different tasting experience for its patrons upon every visit, a steady rotation of limited-edition and seasonal offerings round out the beer lineup. Sodas, tea and coffee are also made on-site to complement the beers. Food trucks frequently satisfy patrons' need for grub as they enjoy their beverage of choice.

Hans Von Biermann is the patriarchal figurehead at Bone Haus, as demonstrated throughout the intricate artwork showcased throughout the brewery. "The catacombs made quite an impression on me and early on we partnered with a Day of the Dead artist named David Lozeau to conceive the tap room and develop the brand," said Chapman. "Once that was established, I worked the story of the brand into the local lore and tied it into the mystery surrounding the Lost Dutchman mine and late 1800s Arizona Territory tales working with a local digital artist, Mikel Whelan."

The beers reflect the brewery's dark theme, including Reaper's Widow Amber Altbier, a German amber altbier. Using a technique known as "wet hopping," which preserves the freshest, most natural essence of the hops, Amarillo varietals are overnighted from Oregon and combined with nine different grains to provide a complex flavor profile, a pleasant aromatic bouquet and a crisp, clean finish. 5.5% ABV, 23 IBU.

Chocolate Porter, 5.5% ABV, 26 IBU, is a creamy, dark ale with balanced chocolate and light roast flavors. Miner's Debt Black India Pale Ale is the brewery's flagship offering. The deep color is derived from dark European grains and exhibits both well-rounded bitterness and hints of mocha. 5.0% ABV, 55 IBU.

Other mainstays in the sixteen-tap lineup include: Double Coffee Milk Stout, Maple Mesquite Brown Ale and lighter beers such as Engelmann's Elixir Prickly Pear Pale Ale and Carbide Light Blonde Ale.

The creativity doesn't stop in the brewhouse. The process of creating the art is just as interesting. "Mikel is predominantly a production artist so I write up a story or scene and he sketches it," said Chapman. "We make changes and then he produces the final art. Each of these stories will be our label art when we begin producing cans."

It didn't take much of a sell for Weiner to convince Chapman to go into business together. "Andy approached me at one of his homebrew sampling

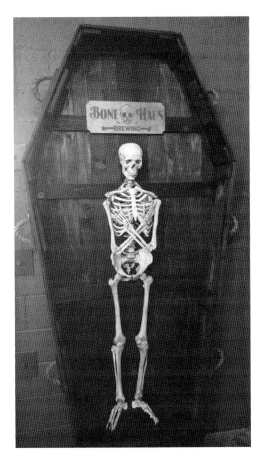

Right: No bones about it.

Below: Bone Haus Brewing tap lineup.

sessions saying he thought I would make a great partner for a new business he had in mind—a microbrewery. Without even really thinking about it, I said 'I'm in.' I was prone to passion industries like music, so I felt right at home with conceiving a brewery with Andy."

Flying Basset Brewing Company

Rob Gagnon knows a little something about flying. Having flown for an airline and for Homeland Security, Gagnon logged many hours in the air. His career provided him with frequent days off, which Gagnon dedicated toward his homebrewing hobby. Brewing as often as possible, Gagnon honed his skills quickly, winning medals. It wasn't long before he started thinking about brewing as a potential profession.

In the midst of his obsession with homebrewing, Gagnon married Sara Cotton. She fully supported Gagnon's idea of opening a bar, and the couple decided it might as well be a brewery. After attending a Master Brewers Association program in Wisconsin to learn about brewery operations in 2012, Gagnon applied for and landed a brewing position at BJ's in Chandler. Working under Derek Osborne, Gagnon inherited the brewing job left vacant by Jeff Huss, who left to pursue opening a brewery of his own.

After brewing at BJ's for a couple years, Gagnon and Cotton moved to Hawaii. The couple thought about opening a brewery in Kauai but quickly found it unfeasible. They moved back to Arizona, drew up a business plan and adopted a basset hound named Lieutenant Dan. Soon after, they found a perfect location just a few miles from bustling downtown Gilbert but at half the rent being off the strip.

Between Gagnon's aviation history and the couple's affinity for their beloved dog, the name Flying Basset was born. As they built out the brewery, they incorporated airplane-themed memorabilia throughout the brewery's interior, including a hostess stand crafted from an airline beverage cart. Flying Basset Brewing Company is a celebration of aviation and canines.

Flying Basset Brewing opened for business on February 8, 2018.

Gagnon drew inspiration from his days at BJ's when developing Flying Basset's flagship beer, the Copper Ale. Having brewed a similar version while at BJs, Gagnon created an amber-colored light-bodied ale that checks in at 4.7% ABV, 25 IBU, possessing caramel and subtle hop notes.

Flying Basset Brewing's Sara Cotton and Rob Gagnon. *Courtesy of Rob Gagnon.*

Light vanilla notes surround the bready malt flavors in Living the Dream Cream Ale, 5.3% ABV, 20 IBU. Tuskegee Red IPA packs a punch at 7.1% ABV, 74 IBU, with hops dominating the flavor and aroma profile. A new addition to the lineup is 747 Heavy, a double IPA that checks in at 8.2% ABV and 80 IBU.

When they are not at the brewery, Rob maintains a part-time job flying for a charter airline in Tucson. Sara remains a full-time RN and ICU manager at a local hospital. The family grew by one when a second basset hound, Angela, joined Lieutenant Dan, rounding out the family.

The family-friendly Flying Basset Brewery has a full menu and full bar. A shuffleboard table, ping pong and cornhole ensure there's always something to do for kids and adults alike. Dogs are welcome on the patio, where basset snacks await the four-legged friends.

Flying Basset Brewing self-distributes draft in locations around the valley and employs Manuel Brothers Distributing to expand its footprint in Flagstaff and Tucson. The sky is the limit for this young brewery making a name for itself in suburban Gilbert, Arizona.

Goldwater Brewing

Greg McClelland is one of those guys who likes to take his time to get it right. First homebrewing in his garage over thirty years ago, McClelland has had the bug for brewing for quite some time, despite taking a while to make it a profession.

McClelland honed his craft at his Mesa home, often with his kids nearby, unknowingly absorbing beer knowledge at an early age. With wife Pam onboard, the couple contemplated opening a brewery long before they actually did, finding neither the timing nor the circumstances ideal the first or second time around.

The dream of brewery ownership gnawed at McClelland for years. When his kids were fully grown and shared his love for craft beer, the time had finally come to finally see the dream through. Goldwater Brewing Company came to fruition in 2015 in the former Scottsdale Auction House building, a place where a young McClelland once bought and sold bicycles.

Middle child and eldest son Chad McClelland is the brewmaster at Goldwater. Having assisted his dad since his younger days, Chad picked up on the nuances needed to brew great beer. Working at a local startup brewery and experiencing various beer cultures while traveling the world have helped transfer his skills from the garage to the commercial level.

Cheers to Goldwater beers. *Courtesy of Goldwater Brewing Company.*

The youngest of Greg and Pam's three kids, Dillon McClelland, specializes in marketing, branding and photography. With a graphic design degree and skills honed from his own independent branding agency, he has a penchant for design and artistic endeavors.

Jimmy Disken became a member of the family after he married the McClelland's eldest child, Treva. A restaurant industry veteran, the "jack of all trades" Disken is Goldwater's general manager, running the taproom as well as handling sales and distribution of the beers.

Desert Rose Cactus Ale, 5.3% ABV, 16 IBU, a crimson red ale, features prickly pear, delivering a true taste of the Southwest. Hop Chowda Hazy IPA, 6.4% ABV, 35 IBU, is a hazy hop bomb with notes of mango and citrus. Scotch'dale, an ode to the city in which the brewery resides, is a 6.6% ABV, 27 IBU Scotch ale.

Located on Scottsdale Road and Goldwater Boulevard, Goldwater Brewing Company offers two taprooms on-site. The main upstairs industrial-contemporary taproom serves up many of the house-made beers on fifteen rotating taps, while the Goldmine Underground Tap & Barrel offers specialty one-off brews and barrel-aged beers sixteen feet underground in the old Mandall's Basement Shooting Range.

Left to right: Greg, Chad and Dillon McClelland and Jimmy Disken of Goldwater Brewing. *Courtesy of Goldwater Brewing Company.*

This Old Town Scottsdale brewery is a shining example of an entrepreneurial family business. With a focus on all things local, Goldwater Brewing produces high-quality beers that exemplify the passion and dedication reflective of the people behind those beers.

While it may have been the elder McClelland who first had the idea to open a brewery, each team member has his or her own personal area of expertise contributing to the brewery's success. No fancy titles or hierarchy exists at Goldwater Brewing. It's just a close-knit family rallying around a love for craft beer; their passion shows in everything they do.

Huss Brewing Company

Jeff and Leah Huss met in a town more than a thousand miles from their respective birth places, as if through an act of serendipity. Brought together by a mutual love of craft beer, they bought an Alaskan Smoked Porter the day they met in December 2005, a bottle that remains in their mini fridge to this day, waiting for the perfect moment to open it. Their intertwining paths to becoming husband-and-wife brewery owners displayed the same patience and determination. As they were willing to put in the time and learn the intricacies of the industry, Huss Brewing has blossomed into one of Arizona's fastest rising stars.

Like most brewers, Jeff Huss did not start out on a beer-related path. Working toward a sales management degree at Purdue University, Jeff didn't really know much about beer, until he discovered a bar called Chumley's that had fifty taps and a "beer passport" program. Being open to trying new styles helped Jeff develop a palate for great beer.

It wasn't long before Jeff discovered a local shop that sold homebrew supplies, piquing his interest in the craft. The shop, Grape and Grain, was located in Springfield, Illinois, about a forty-five-minute drive. It just so happened that Springfield was also home to an aspiring craft beer aficionado named Leah Ryan.

With a waning interest in sales management and a growing interest in homebrewing, Jeff sought out opportunities to learn about beer. Deciding he'd rather pursue beer than work in corporate America, Jeff applied, and was accepted to, Chicago's Siebel Brewing Academy.

In 2005, there weren't as many brewing opportunities as there are today. Jeff had difficulty finding the right job. Frustrated, Jeff decided to clear his head with a visit to see his sister in Scottsdale. His parents encouraged

Jeff and Leah Huss, founders of Huss Brewing. *Courtesy of Huss Brewing.*

him to apply to at least one company while he was there, even if just for the experience.

Leah had a cross-country adventure of her own trying to figure out exactly what she wanted to do and where. In the mid-1990s, she left the cold winters of Springfield and relocated to Arizona, where she worked a number of jobs in the hospitality industry. A common theme she encountered in these establishments was the focus on providing good craft beer.

She spent time working for Uptown Brewery in Scottsdale as a waitress while she attended culinary school. She spent a lot of time at a place called Timberwolf that had seventy-five different draft beers, which helped Leah develop her understanding of different beer styles. Sierra Nevada Pale Ale was her old faithful, but she was eager to try any new beer she could. Little did she realize the craft beer jackpot just ahead on her horizon.

After graduating culinary school, Leah embarked on a unique opportunity to be a chef on a private charter yacht in Alaska. When that seasonal opportunity concluded, she returned to Arizona in the summer of 2001. As she initially had difficulty finding a job in Arizona, a friend recommended checking out a new spot called Papago Brewing.

Papago hired Leah that day. One of the owners, a beer connoisseur named Ron Kloth, was impressed with Leah's beer knowledge and became her unofficial mentor. She became manager, then general manager, before eventually becoming a partner.

Jeff followed through on his word and scheduled an interview while on his trip to Arizona. Wanting to become a professional brewer, he made connections with Derek "Doc" Osborne at BJ's, a new brewery located in Chandler, Arizona. Osborne had been with the company from the beginning but was newly settled in Arizona, opening the new BJ's facility. He had an assistant but needed another hand to help with miscellaneous brewery tasks.

Osborne offered Jeff Huss a position as a part-time assistant. Loving the weather and with no other prospects on the horizon, he accepted the position. It was a start in the brewing field.

Coincidently, Kloth happened to be at BJ's that very day that Jeff interviewed. Serendipity struck when Osborne, Huss and Kloth ended up having a conversation. Jeff was excited to finally land a job in the brewing field but had concerns that it was only part-time hours. Kloth suggested he go see his general manager, Leah, at Papago Brewing, and maybe she'd be able to help him out with some additional part-time hours as a bartender.

Jeff didn't go to Papago, at least not immediately. Within weeks of being hired, the brewer Jeff was assisting was let go, catapulting Jeff to become Osborne's main assistant. The hours became full time, and Jeff had the job he trained for at the Siebel Brewing Academy. Later that year, Jeff and Leah finally met, but only in passing.

It wasn't until Jeff and Leah crossed paths at the Arizona Strong Beer Fest 2006 that they finally had a lengthy, in-depth conversation about beer, their Midwest roots and life in general. The two hit it off. They began to date and married two years later. A couple of beer-obsessed midwesterners who grew up forty-five minutes apart met, fell in love and got married in the southwestern desert. Hollywood couldn't have scripted it any better.

Jeff enjoyed his time working at BJ's, learning from one of Arizona's best brewmasters in Osborne, all the while learning the ins and outs of the brewing business. Leah continued to make Papago Brewing a destination place for any craft beer lover.

All along, Jeff's endgame was to open a brewery of his own. Early on, he and his brother Mark talked about opening a place. While those talks didn't progress, a friendship turned into a partnership with Brian Dewey, a sales rep for Sierra Nevada Brewing Company. Like Jeff, Brian was a diehard

It's all about family at Huss Brewing. *Courtesy of Huss Brewing.*

craft-beer enthusiast and saw the limitless opportunities craft beer could provide. The two talked often and started devising plans for a brewery under the working name Legend City Brewing Company.

Now settled in as head brewer at BJ's, Jeff learned an amazing amount from Doc Osborne and the entire BJ's experience. At a certain point, Jeff felt as if he went as far as BJs could take him. By this time, he had learned brewing, filtering, accounting—virtually everything except packaging. After seven years of making some of Arizona's best beer, Jeff gave twelve weeks' notice and left BJ's in February 2013.

While Jeff was clearly on a path to brewery ownership, it was not to be with Brian Dewey, who moved his family to California. Jeff needed a plan B.

In a recurring theme, Jeff and Leah again found themselves at the Strong Beer Festival. Pregnant at the time, Leah was not only the designated driver, she was also contemplating the family's future. She and Jeff had a heart-to-heart talk at the event, and the two decided to go into business together. She had extensive experience running a highly successful business in Papago, and he did his due diligence learning the brewing side. A new brewery was born.

Arguably one of the most unassuming people in the brewing industry, Jeff was apprehensive about naming a brewery after himself. Realizing it was going to be a family effort, and knowing how difficult it is to find a nontrademarked name, he figured, why not just use the name Huss?

While Huss Brewing was still in the planning stages, an agreement was reached with Papago ownership to take over production of two of its popular beers: Orange Blossom and Coconut Joe. Having this agreement already established ensured Jeff could start with a built-in demand and gave him the confidence to build his brewery to the specifications he originally envisioned.

Orange Blossom was originally created when Leah, Ron and other members of Papago's staff sat together adjusting levels of vanilla and mandarin in a basic wheat beer until the desired profile was achieved. First brewed via a contract agreement by Scott Yarosh at Sonoran Brewing, later, Papago's beers were brewed by Phoenix's Sun Up Brewing and Sedona's Oak Creek Brewing, before Huss Brewing eventually took over production. Wildly popular, Papago Orange Blossom is the number-two-selling beer produced in the state of Arizona, trailing only Four Peaks' Kilt Lifter.

Before Jeff could brew his or Papago's beers, he needed to build a brewery. Construction started in May 2013. Without full-time employment at the time, Jeff was anxious to open as soon as possible. Huss Brewing opened first as a bar on August 23, 2013, after receiving a certificate of occupancy. When local, state and federal inspections were complete and approvals granted, Jeff Huss brewed the first batch of Huss Brewing beer, That'll Do IPA, in September. The first beer was sold in October 2013.

Jeff recalled, "We had a tiny supply of hops. That'll Do IPA was meant to be a one time, one-and-done beer. We ended up brewing it continuously for four years."

When he got into the brewing business, Jeff expected to be predominantly a hops-forward brewery, since IPAs and pale ales were all the rage. "I figured we'd be an IPA brewery, and I never expected to make as many light beers as we do. Scottsdale Blonde is our flagship and biggest seller, a really great beer for our hot-weather climate," he said.

Leah spent fourteen years as general manager and partner with Papago, having access to every beer that passed through the state of Arizona. "I went through all the extremes," Leah said. "I love a beer that is clean and flawless. We like to have several beers at a sitting, so I tend to respect a well-made, lighter beer," she said.

While Huss Brewing continues to grow, now the third-largest brewer in Arizona, it's not all about huge growth for the Huss family. "We're not trying

Fresh Huss on tap. *Courtesy of Huss Brewing.*

to be crazy popular; we just want to do things the right way," said Leah. "We believe in business ethics. We make everyone in our organization feel like they are part of our family."

Whether or not they strive for growth, it's happening. Things are on the rise all around for Huss Brewing Company. Working with Crescent

Crown Distributing, which acquired Little Guy Distributing years earlier, has been a perfect fit for Huss Brewing. The distributor grew the brand quickly and effectively. When Huss began canning, it took everything to a whole new level.

Having been a draft-only option up to that point, Huss was the first brewery to can Papago beers. The first run of Papago Orange Blossom called for one hundred cases to be canned. Eighty-two cases were sold at Papago Brewing the very first evening they were available.

Huss had a brewing agreement in place that would ensure production of the Papago brands through 2018. However, talks ensued, and an agreement was reached between the Huss family and the Papago owners to purchase the permanent rights to all Papago Brewing beers. Leah had come full circle.

Starting as a bartender, working her way to partner, relinquishing that role, then eventually owning the brand she originally helped create, Leah was involved in some way, shape or form throughout the whole process.

All of Huss Brewing's beers are made at its Tempe production facility, the former site of the defunct Rio Salado Brewing Company. With just a modest taproom, Leah and Jeff soon realized that the brewery needed to have a true "face."

After they opened a tasting room in Uptown Phoenix at Camelback and Central, fans of Huss Brewing could enjoy Huss and Papago beers, have a delicious meal and relax in comfort. Whether it's inside the welcoming taproom or outdoors on the view-filled patio, Huss Brewing's Uptown location is "ground zero" for the craft brewing scene in Arizona.

While Orange Blossom is technically the brewery's no. 1 seller, Scottsdale Blonde holds the honor of no. 1 seller within the Huss portfolio. At 4.7% ABV and 18 IBU, this Kolsch-style beer is light and perfect for the Arizona heat. Cult favorite Koffee Kolsch uses Scottsdale Blonde as its base, with the captivating addition of real coffee. Similar to That'll Do IPA, the beer was intended to be a one-off for Craft 64's second anniversary party. The party and the beer were huge hits, and the beer became part of the regular lineup.

Copper State IPA started out as an experimental batch, trying to capture the essence of leading IPAs, with a Huss twist. After two or three iterations, Copper State was dialed in and is wildly popular, featuring its Simcoe, Zythos and Citra symphony of hops.

Magic in the Ivy is an ode to Jeff's favorite place on earth, Wrigley Field, where he believed magic truly existed. When his beloved Cubs won it all in 2016, he knew he was right.

Service with a smile at Huss Brewing.

Copper State IPA. *Courtesy of Huss Brewing.*

All about making a difference in the community and leaving a legacy for their family, Jeff and Leah Huss do things the right way. It's all about quality, people and community. Leah runs the company, and Jeff runs the brewing operation. Their complementary skill sets work well to make Huss Brewing as successful as it can be and likely will continue to be for years to come.

Huss Brewing was recognized for its quality when it won a gold medal at the prestigious Great American Beer Festival for its Husstler Milk Stout, right about the time Jeff and Leah were celebrating ten years of being in each other's lives. Had they not been in Denver, maybe they would have finally cracked open that bottle of Alaskan Smoked Porter. For now, it remains in the fridge, presumably getting better with age, just like the brewery that shares the family name.

Huss American Lager.

Lochiel Brewing

Dedication to history and heritage is the drive behind Lochiel Brewing Company of Mesa. Owner/brewer Ian Cameron delves into his Scottish lineage, crafting a beer lineup reminiscent of those found in and around his ancestral homeland. Lochiel is an extension of Cameron's family's name, Cameron of Lochiel. Several recipes employed at Lochiel Brewing are family recipes passed down for generations.

In addition to the Scottish lineage, there is also an Arizona connection. According to Cameron, the small town of Lochiel, Arizona, was founded in the 1800s by a cattle baron named Colin Cameron, a distant cousin. Cameron highlights his mostly European-style recipes with a couple Mexican-influenced ones to pay homage to both family histories.

Cameron professes to have brewed alcoholic beverages from a very early age, assisting older family members on anything from beer to naturally fermented root beer. Honing his focus on traditional beer in his later teenage years, he perfected many of his recipes by the time he was in his early twenties, despite brewing on rudimentary equipment.

At age twenty-three, he upgraded to a one-barrel professional-style system, which provided Cameron the experience of replicating commercial brewing on a smaller scale. In his later twenties, Cameron spent about three years volunteering at a few Phoenix-area breweries, trading his labor for professional experience.

Having spent time in Fort Collins, Colorado, and Albuquerque, New Mexico, before settling in Arizona, Cameron observed various breweries throughout the years. These experiences helped him envision his own future brewery. Honing this vision while gaining real-life experience volunteering locally gave Cameron the confidence he needed to take the leap on his own.

Besides the years of hands-on brewing, Cameron had another distinct advantage when it came to brewing: a thorough understanding of water chemistry. Since beer is over 90 percent water, having the proper water is the foundation upon which any good beer is built.

Having previously worked in the water department for SRP, Cameron had knowledge about which areas had the cleanest natural water source. Armed with that information, he set out to open his brewery in East Mesa, where fresh water could be sourced from the Rio Salado and the Lost Dutchman Spring, providing an optimal water profile that could create great beer.

Banking enough money by age thirty-two to fund his project, he made the jump into brewery ownership. Fully determined to make his dream a

Ian Cameron, Lochiel Brewing. *Courtesy of Jill McNamara.*

reality, Cameron secured a location and went to work—by himself. Doing everything from construction to plumbing and wiring, along with all the legal documentation for licensure, he kept the project on track, continuously moving forward. Lochiel Brewing opened for business in May 2015.

By taking on so much of the work himself, Cameron was able to stick to a strict budget, get the place up and running and operating profitably, without debt, by year two.

Lochiel's no. 1 seller is the Scotch Ale, which checks in at 8.7% ABV and 30 IBU. Reinterpreting a three-hundred-year-old family recipe that called for fermentation in oak barrels, Cameron was the first of nine generations able to adapt the recipe to stainless-steel brewing equipment.

Lochiel's Extra Special Bitter (ESB) is an easy-drinking 5.5% ABV and 35 IBU ale. Crafted in the style of a malty pale ale, this beer can be enjoyed in quantity. The Porter packs a punch at 6.9% ABV and 41 IBU, blurring the line between stout and porter.

The Narcocorrido Mexican Lager also comes from family recipes. Using a combination of Pilsner, Vienna and Scottish grains, with a Mexican lager hopping schedule, the beer is an ode to the southwestern lineage of the Cameron family in Arizona.

Cameron has accomplished a lot in a relatively short period of time. Having worked in a variety of fields such as contracting, aerospace engineering and cyber counterterrorism, he's had a wide range of experiences that all played a role in getting him to where he is today. The fact that he has been able to accomplish these things speaks to his dedication and his work ethic. Considering he's been able to do all this without the gift of hearing makes Cameron's accomplishments all the more impressive and awe-inspiring.

McFate (Fate) Brewing Company

Call it destiny, call it fate. Or maybe call it McFate? Whatever you call Steve McFate's Scottsdale breweries, one thing is certain: this is some of the best beer made in Arizona.

Steve McFate started his craft beer journey enjoying mostly European and Belgian ales, which inspired him to eventually take up the challenge of brewing his own beer. Steve calls this his "awakening."

After taking up homebrewing, it didn't take long for Steve to figure out how much work went into making a simple batch of homebrew. While the beer industry appealed to him as a whole, from the unique flavors, the beer culture, to the sights and sounds of being in a brewpub setting, the pull wasn't strong enough to get him to leave his day job—yet.

He had a career in finance, mainly mortgage lending. McFate started out as a real estate appraiser; it was a demanding job. It took a lot of hours, required an immense amount of driving and was not much fun. Arizona was booming, and Steve was always busy. While anything but relaxing, the industry provided a steady paycheck and satisfied his interest in analytics.

He later became a loan officer, which led to him opening a company called America's Mortgage Alliance. Partnering with a childhood friend, their boutique operation had modest success even after the great recession of 2007. Despite these successes, Steve still felt a need for something more meaningful.

Torn between wanting to find purpose and simply wanting to go to work every day in shorts and a T-shirt, McFate was at a crossroads. Sometimes it's the little things that matter most.

Knowing opportunities were out there somewhere, Steve decided to take a one-year sabbatical to figure out what to do with the rest of his life. While he didn't yet know what that was, he was pretty confident it wasn't working in the mortgage lending business.

Steve McFate, founder, McFate Brewing. *Courtesy of Steve McFate.*

Taking full advantage of his year away from work, Steve traveled all over the country. The beer bug caught up with him again. During his travels, he visited as many breweries and met as many people in the brewing industry as possible. He wanted to gauge whether or not brewing was a viable career option, and if it was, he needed to know what it would take.

Steve's travels found him in Ridgway, Colorado, where he met Tom Hennessy, known for his expertise in consulting aspiring brewers on how to open breweries on limited budgets. Hennessy runs a renowned course called the Brewery Immersion Course at the Colorado Boy Pub & Brewery he owned. Steve and Tom immediately became fast friends.

During the course, Steve learned different aspects of the brewing business, not just brewing. He learned about brewery budgets and how to operate a professional business. Brewing was coming into focus as a viable career option.

A career-altering event happened when Hennessy contacted Steve with an opportunity to come work for him. Having come to the end of his one-year sabbatical, Steve talked with his business partner, and they decided to part ways, with Steve selling his portion of the business to his partner.

In what became almost a second sabbatical, Steve learned under Hennessy, this time for an entire year, instead of just a week, and had the opportunity to truly absorb the nuances and plot twists that occur as a brewery operator. After a year working for Hennessy, Steve knew it was time to make a serious career move. It was January 2012, and brewing was the path he decided to pursue.

Having not worked in the "real world" now for two years, Steve put his efforts into high gear. He first considered property in downtown Phoenix but later made the decision to be closer to his home in Scottsdale. Fate Brewing Company was established and opened on November 12, 2012, on Shea Boulevard near Scottsdale Road.

The location was perfect. As it had previously housed a restaurant, the facility could easily be converted into a brewpub. Incidentally, this was one of the prerequisites that Hennessy taught Steve during his Brewery Immersion Course—find a former restaurant location to save big money on buildout.

A lease was signed in April and much of the work was performed by Steve, friends and family. Building tables by hand, they took the concept of "hand-crafted" to a whole new level.

At that time, banks wouldn't touch a first-time entrepreneur wanting to get into the restaurant industry, so Steve kept to a strict budget and continued to do as much as he could do on his own. He scoured sources for brewing equipment such as Probrewer.com, but he was in serious competition for equipment. Breweries were popping up across the country like dandelions after the first good spring rain.

In a bit of luck, he found a post selling a seven-barrel mash tun and brew kettle. The equipment was sitting in storage in Albuquerque, New Mexico. Quickly purchasing a plane ticket, Steve went to check it out and immediately put down a deposit. He now had the building and the brewing equipment.

A few weeks later, Steve rented a trailer to go pick up the equipment. Serendipity struck again when, while in Albuquerque, Steve noticed another post from a brewery in Silverton, Colorado, that was selling serving tanks. Wasting no time, he contacted the brewery and agreed to buy them, sight unseen.

He explained that he needed to drive his newly bought equipment back to Phoenix first, then he would make his way up to Silverton. As it turned out, there was no need. While the brewery was located in Colorado, the brewer was storing the tanks at his parent's house—in Albuquerque. Ecstatic, Steve made room in the trailer and eventually drove back to Phoenix with not only his mash tun and kettle but also six serving vessels, known as Grundy tanks.

Having friends in the local community paid immediate dividends. Friends at Four Peaks, who were well versed in Grundy tanks, had the parts Steve needed to make the serving tanks functional. It wouldn't be the last time the two breweries collaborated. Six months after opening, Fate and Four Peaks collaborated to produce a beer together.

Despite years of homebrewing experience and the full year working closely with Tom Hennessy, Steve still wasn't unequivocally confident in his ability to run both the brewhouse and the business. He decided to seek out a full-time brewer to handle the brewing duties. He came across a post on one of the beer industry sites and found a brewer from upstate New York named Adam Schmeichel. Brewing at Adirondack Brewing Company at the time, Adam was interested in relocating to a warmer climate. Steve had close friends in the area where Adam worked so he had them conduct a live interview on his behalf.

The reviews of Adam and his beers came back with flying colors, and he was hired to be the head brewer of the new Fate Brewing Company without actually meeting Steve in person. He arrived in the valley about a month later and has held the post ever since.

Originally from a small town in southwest Michigan called Berrien Springs, Schmeichel went to culinary school in Hyde Park, New York, at the famed Culinary Institute of America. He began homebrewing toward the end of his studies.

Moving back home after graduation, he got a job in a small brewery in Michigan known as Round Barn Brewing Company. In exchange for running the café, he got to work in the brewery, winery and distillery. Following this stint, he moved back to upstate New York and took the job at Adirondack Brewery in Lake George, where he brewed from 2007 to 2012. Adam followed his passion for brewing, which actually superseded his passion for cooking. He turned out to be the missing piece needed to complete McFate's team.

With all the pieces in place, Steve assembled his brewery, put together his taproom and pizza kitchen and went through all the necessary permitting and licensure. On November 12, 2012, Fate Brewing Company was opened for business. Fate served up light fare, including pizzas and pretzels, along with house beers and a few guest taps.

In September 2013, Fate Brewing won a silver medal at the prestigious Great American Beer Festival for its Candy Bar Milk Stout. Business boomed after that big win.

The relatively small brewery found immediate success and was packed a majority of the time. The beer went fast and furiously. At times, the brewery would be down to as little as three house beers and have to augment the lineup with local guest beers just to have something to serve the thirsty patrons.

It became apparent that, to meet demand, a bigger space was needed. The search began for a larger space. At the time when Fate Brewing opened, there were about thirty breweries operating in Arizona. That number has more than tripled and shows no signs of slowing down. The climate is hot, and the locals crave their beer to help keep them cool.

The search didn't take Steve very far. A large fifteen-thousand-square-foot building was available in the southern end of Scottsdale, eleven thousand square feet of which could serve all the needs of the brewery. While Steve initially was looking exclusively for warehouse space, not looking to open a second restaurant, the opportunity that presented itself on the highly traveled Scottsdale Road was too much to pass up.

The developer Steve was working with, Tom Frenkel, was also an investor, and although Steve was the sole owner of Fate Brewing Company, he knew he would need to take on a partner if he wanted to swing this new facility, three times the size of his current location. He and Frenkel became business partners, and Fate Brewing South opened in August 2015.

A bit of irony occurred during the search for the second location. Having grown up in Scottsdale and being an avid biker as a kid, Steve was a member

McFate South at night. *Courtesy of McFate Brewing.*

of a local bike club that traveled around town. Each ride would conclude at a particular restaurant where the kids' parents would pick them up. As it turned out, the very building that became Fate South was one of the stops Steve made during many of his biking excursions. It was a "coming full circle" experience for Steve, having visited the place as a kid and now being the proprietor.

Fate's success in the beer industry came quickly and did not go unnoticed. In fact, it caught the attention of Fate Brewing of Colorado, which did not appreciate having another brewery west of the Mississippi using the same name. Rather than going to court and going through lengthy legal proceedings, the two Fate Brewing Companies came to a resolution that resulted in Steve changing the name Fate to McFate. This change took place officially in June 2016.

Both locations continue to have great success, and the beers continue to be recognized for their quality. The brewery won a prestigious Gold Medal at the 2018 World Beer Cup for its popular Hatch Chile Gatos, a true taste of the Southwest. A cream ale, Hatch Chile Gatos is made with peppers from Hatch, New Mexico. The light-bodied beer has a wonderfully clean, crisp pepper taste with little to no heat, making it a wonderful warm weather beer.

While the brew staff of four enjoy introducing new flavors and styles to keep things interesting, some regular house beers set the standard for their respective styles. The Irish Red is crafted true to the original red ales made famous in Ireland. Similarly, the Vienna Lager hits the mark for authenticity with rich, toasty Vienna malt and a smooth, refreshing finish.

The "cold weather" seasonal, Candy Bar Milk Stout, wows beer geeks and beer newbies alike with its flavors and aromas reminiscent of chocolate milk.

According to Steve, being able to just be himself is what is most satisfying. "It's such a luxury to be able to show up in jeans and T-shirt to work," he affirmed. "Really, the most important thing is to be able to do something that you enjoy. We all need to make a living doing something. Who wouldn't prefer to work over a beer?"

After independently founding the company in 2012, Steve sold the operations to Frenkel in early 2019. Steve is actively pursuing a new, yet unnamed project at press time, while Frenkel worked out a deal to change the brewery name back to Fate Brewing Company, the name it operates under today.

O.H.S.O. Brewery

Grand Rapids, Michigan transplant Jon Lane wanted to escape the frigid winters and gray gloom of the Midwest. Relocating to Gilbert, Arizona, in 1990, Lane had developed a love for craft beer and homebrewing and was strongly considering entering the industry.

Envisioning opening a craft beer bar, Lane connected with fellow enthusiast Pat Walsh, and the two eventually decided to become business partners. Plans shifted, and the partners decided to open a brewery instead of a straightforward craft beer bar. O.H.S.O. was born when Lane and Walsh connected with a consultant who was the missing piece needed to get the project off the ground.

Lane took charge of everything to do with the beer, food and marketing needs of the business. Walsh managed the day-to-day operations, while the consultant was instrumental in the construction of the restaurant.

Opening a business can stretch a person's limits, especially a budget. In Lane's case, it reached an extreme when, in an effort to generate income, he rented out his condo, effectively relegating him to live in his office with his six-year-old son Owen for eight patience-testing weeks. With credit cards

O.H.S.O.'s Jon Lane. *Courtesy of Jon Lane.*

maxed and no looking back, Lane and Walsh opened O.H.S.O. Brewery in Arcadia on November 15, 2011. A laser-focused, never-give-up attitude made opening the doors possible.

O.H.S.O. stands for Outrageous Homebrewers' Social Outpost. While certainly not a homebrew club, the brewery encourages homebrewers and beer enthusiasts to learn all they can about the brewing process and maybe even participate in brewing a batch.

The mission behind the brewery is to encourage beer education, in part by having an observable brewhouse. According to Lane, "You rarely see people working in breweries. We wanted people to witness beer being brewed to create curiosity about the brewing process. Our classes get people interested and engaged," said Lane. O.H.S.O. offers patrons the chance to participate in an actual brew day, with the resulting brews going on tap in the brewery.

While Walsh loved O.H.S.O. and the people involved with it, he had interests outside of the restaurant and made the decision to pursue other endeavors. Selling his shares to Lane, Walsh became a flight medic, and Lane became O.H.S.O.'s sole owner.

Despite Lane's resilience, running O.H.S.O. was no walk in the park. In fact, recurring sinus issues prevented Lane from realizing that the beers being produced in his brewery were sometimes flawed. Three sinus-related surgeries later, Lane recovered his ability to smell and taste and was surprised at what he discovered.

"At first, our beer just wasn't that good, but I was totally unaware of this because of my inability to properly smell and taste the beer," said Lane.

He hired a new brewer with a strong attention to detail, especially regarding cleaning and sanitizing processes. Things began to improve, taking about a year to achieve the desired level of quality. Patrons who shied away from the brewery began to come back as positive word-of-mouth traveled. Lane instituted an official training program for his brew staff to ensure they were constantly learning and improving.

Brewing on a small system that produced just three kegs at a time, O.H.S.O. filled out the tap lineup with a mix of its own beers and local Arizona beers. From day one, O.H.S.O. has been huge supporters of the local brewing scene.

In May 2013, with recipes locked and loaded and processes dialed in, Lane sought to expand. Finding an ideal space in Paradise Valley, Lane signed a lease for O.H.S.O.'s second location.

Delay after delay slowed, then halted, progress on the new location. Lane grew impatient and began to look for other locations. He found a highly visible space in North Scottsdale, walking distance from a Four Peaks brewpub.

With the Paradise Valley project effectively in limbo, Lane signed the lease to open his second location in North Scottsdale. Keenly aware that he was opening in the same plaza as Arizona's most popular brewery, Lane alertly decided to make distilling a focal point of the Scottsdale location. Plans for a distillery were drawn, and construction began.

Distilling was still a fairly new concept in Arizona, and laws were still evolving. Wanting to open a public-facing distillery in the spirit of his Arcadia brewery, Lane came to find in the eleventh hour that the laws did not allow this idea. To have a distillery, law dictated it had to be in a separate facility with an entirely separate entryway.

Already committed to the plan, Lane had to lease a separate parcel to accommodate the distillery. The size and budget of the project tripled. Undeterred, Lane opened the North Scottsdale O.H.S.O. in April 2014.

With little time to celebrate the opening of Scottsdale, the Paradise Valley location, still under signed lease, was finally ready for build out. Jumping back into construction mode, Lane forged ahead and Paradise Valley became O.H.S.O. number three, the second of which to be designed as a brewpub.

Midway through the process, the space next door became available, allowing Paradise Valley to have significantly more square footage along with a desirable huge patio. Lane bit the bullet and took on the additional space. Paradise Valley opened in March 2015, making O.H.S.O. a force in the Phoenix brewing scene. Lane had come a long way in a short period of time. The man who lived in his office for a time now owned three of the area's most popular establishments.

Content with his thriving hot spots and having no intention of further expansion, Lane was approached by a developer who had a perfect opportunity in growing downtown Gilbert, Lane's first Arizona hometown. Tapped out financially, but envisioning the potential in the area, Lane took on his first loan and opened O.H.S.O.'s fourth location in downtown Gilbert in April 2018.

Making necessary sacrifices along the way, Lane went one and a half years without taking a paycheck. When he did finally pay himself, he took only what he needed to cover bills. For Lane, it's the business ownership experience that drives him. "Even five years into the business, I wasn't making what I used to make in the chain-restaurant world," said Lane.

Being an active member of the community is one of the things Lane loves most. O.H.S.O. regularly holds fundraising events for kids, teachers and pets, giving back to the community that has embraced the brewery. Throughout the year, O.H.S.O. hands out ten thousand gift certificates to Phoenix-area teachers for a complimentary lunch as the company's way of saying "thank you."

The brewery that once made beer on a glorified homebrewing system has come a long way. The tap lineup now includes lagers and barrel-aged beers. The distilling part of the business is also thriving.

Popcycle Blonde is perfectly crafted for the Arizona sun. At just 4.5% ABV and 8 IBU, this light and sweet ale combines lemons and raspberries to create the perfect thirst quencher. 89Ale is an ode to an American classic style, the California Common, originally created during the gold rush. Amber in color, 89Ale possesses dark toasty bread notes that complement toffee and caramel flavors. Lost Viking is a Baltic Porter, a complex beer style with notes of smoke and chocolate, which are mellowed due to an extended lagering period, creating a smooth, flavorful dark beer.

Lane has rolled the dice more than once and came out victorious. "If I had it to do over again, I might change a few things. I would invest in technology sooner and make education for my workers an even bigger priority because learning helps them grow," said Lane. "But I'd definitely do it all over again."

Old Ellsworth Brewing Company

Old Ellsworth may be a family affair, but none of the family is named Ellsworth. The brainchild of the husband-and-wife team of Brian and Christine "Chris" McKean and Chris's brother Ryan Bostrom, the name is an ode to Ellsworth Road, the street on which the brewery is located.

The journey to Queen Creek, Arizona, was a long one. Brian and Chris decided to seek adventure, splitting their time over nine years working in Skagway, Alaska, in the summer and Cabo San Lucas, Mexico, in the winter. During that time, Brian discovered homebrewing.

In 2009, they came back to Arizona and went to work in different fields. Chris worked for a lawyer's office, Ryan worked for a water purifying company and Brian earned a master's degree in business and a certificate in project management. Little did they realize how these experiences would later affect them opening their brewery. The entire time he was studying for school, Delavan, Illinois native Brian was also intently studying the brewing industry.

The trio talked about opening a brewery and searched for the right opportunity. Ryan saw an ad from the Town of Queen Creek, which was looking to attract a brewery. While viewing potential properties, the group talked with the economic development committee, which mapped out the steps needed to open a brewery in Queen Creek. They looked at an old carniceria, quickly determining it wasn't the right space. However, directly across the street was a restaurant that was exactly what they envisioned.

Shortly thereafter, Brian got a call from the economic development department that the restaurant they liked had become available but would likely be a hot commodity. Working in Phoenix at the time, Brian hopped on his motorcycle, swiftly made the trek to Queen Creek to view the property and, that evening, verbally agreed to take possession.

The three continued to work their full-time jobs and build out the brewery in their limited spare time. Through sheer determination, the sleep-deprived trio opened Old Ellsworth Brewing Company in July 2017, fifteen months after signing the lease.

Old Ellsworth was not the original name of the brewery, however. Originally considering Rittenhouse Brewing Company, they discovered a whiskey of the same name existed, creating a potential conflict with both companies operating within the alcoholic beverage industry. Chris suggested Old Ellsworth, and the brewery had its name.

Even though Old Ellsworth opened in July 2017, it didn't brew its first batch of beer until February 2018 due to equipment issues. The business persevered due to its fine full-service kitchen led by Chef Robert Hutton and an assortment of Arizona-brewed beers that filled the taps.

Cleveland, Ohio native Hutton puts a modern American interpretation on traditional cuisine, producing menu items that included Philly cheesesteak egg rolls, Hatch green chile chicken nachos and a "pick your poutine" option where patrons decide between fries or tots then pick their sauce and toppings.

The twelve-tap lineup features eight house beers, including Legends Never Die, a hazy New England–style IPA. The brewery's no. 1 selling beer, all the hops are added after the boil is complete, which preserves much of the desired hop flavor and aroma.

Erik's Ale, named after Ryan and Chris's grandfather, came from an old Mexican-lager recipe that Old Ellsworth reinterpreted into an ale. Winnie's

A delicious entrée from the kitchen of Old Ellsworth. *Courtesy of O.E.B.C.*

Revenge is a monster of a beer, an imperial saison made with local honey that clocks in at 11% ABV. A Norwegian yeast strain gives Winnie's a unique "farmhouse funk character" sought after by saison aficionados.

Although Brian was the first to brew, he mentored Ryan, who eventually became the head brewer. Chris wears multiple hats, including handling payroll, accounting, social media and running events. Brian is involved in virtually all aspects of the business in some capacity.

Old Ellsworth was named "Emerging Business of the Year" by the Queen Creek Chamber of Commerce.

The camaraderie within the brewing industry is something cherished by the partners. Before Old Ellsworth was equipped to brew, local breweries offered collaboration opportunities so the fledgling business could still have "house" beer on tap. Collaborations with O.H.S.O., North Mountain and Uncle Bear's helped fill the gaps until the brewing system was ready.

That spirit of camaraderie is now coming full circle, as aspiring brewers are reaching out to the team at Old Ellsworth looking for guidance and advice, something the team is more than happy to accommodate.

Oro Brewing Company

"The Spanish word *oro* translates to English as 'gold,'" explained Oro Brewing owner Chuck Wennerlund. Reaching for the gold is the mantra and vision of the company. "To us, this simply means to always be trying to improve ourselves, our business and our community," he said.

Oro Brewing opened its doors in October 2016 with a mix of house beers and local guest beers. Located in downtown Mesa, head brewer Jesse Kortepeter brews on a modest three-barrel system that provides the flexibility to create new and exciting recipes while ensuring the beers remain fresh.

Wennerlund and his good friend Dave Valencia envisioned going into business together. At first, they weren't sure exactly what type of business they'd pursue. They knew it needed to be equal parts fun and meaningful. The two often discussed this subject during homebrewing sessions. While ideas came and went, the beer was the constant, and opening a brewery eventually became their joint venture.

Located in the bustling, artsy downtown Mesa corridor, Oro has a modest rectangular space with an L-shaped bar that encourages conversation among its patrons. With no kitchen at the brewery, Oro teams up with Worth Takeaway next door to provide scratch-made sandwiches for the taproom. This symbiotic relationship provides a brewpub-like feel while eliminating the need for Oro to install its own kitchen.

Hops are in the spotlight at Oro, led by Hop-iphany IPA, All or Nothing Black IPA and Singularity Pale Ale. Each beer has its own character that showcases various hop varietals.

Wennerlund's personal favorite is Hop-iphany, checking in at 7.0% ABV and 70 IBU. The All or Nothing double black IPA, 8.5% ABV, 85 IBU, provides a cacophony of flavors and aromas. Singularity is a single-hop series of pale ales at 5.5% ABV and 45 IBU that is brewed always using the same base style, with each version showcasing a different hop varietal.

Oro also features malt-forward styles for those not as obsessed with all things hops. Inside the Park Blonde Ale is a straightforward, easy-drinking blonde for those looking for something light and approachable. The London Porter is a traditional British porter with notes of chocolate and subtle roast. The unmistakable spicy yeast takes center stage in the Saison, one of the highlights of Kortepeter's lineup.

"I preach continuous improvement," said Kortepeter. "There's always something to learn and ways to improve. You don't have to reinvent the wheel as long as you know how to manufacture a great wheel."

Jesse Kortepeter, head brewer, Oro Brewing Company.

An outdoor patio provides prime people-watching opportunities on the vibrant downtown Main Street strip. Being conveniently located directly off the light rail expands Oro's customer base beyond its loyal locals.

Oro was immediately embraced by the Mesa community. "We thought we were getting into the beer business, but we discovered we're actually in the relationship business first and foremost," said Wennerlund.

"We continue to support our local community with our Community Tap Project," Wennerlund explained. "Proceeds from an Oro beer each month go to a local nonprofit, charity or great cause within the downtown Mesa area. This is an opportunity for our friends and guests to give back and pay it forward to downtown Mesa."

With a wide range of quality-made beer styles, a comfortable setting, a talented brewer and a friendly staff, it's no wonder why Oro Brewing has established itself as a fixture in the reborn downtown Mesa entertainment scene.

Papago Brewing

"Lighten up, it's just beer," quipped the affable Ron Kloth, considered by many to be the godfather of Phoenix's craft beer scene. Kloth was reacting to negative backlash after a light-hearted April Fool's prank at his iconic Scottsdale craft beer watering hole, Papago Brewing. While Kloth may not take himself too seriously, there is little question of the serious impact he and his partners at Papago Brewing had in changing the Phoenix area craft-beer landscape.

It can be argued that every great idea starts with two simple words: "what if?" In the case of three friends who shared a love of craft beer, it turned into a business that was destined to become a Phoenix icon.

Back in 2000, after spending about six months traveling in Europe, primarily in Belgium and Germany, Ron Kloth was exposed to an entirely new world of beer and beer culture. Upon returning to Arizona, he paid a visit to Paul Gunn, the owner of GunnBrew Homebrewing Supplies. Kloth shared his stories of what he had just experienced abroad. The two discussed the idea of having a homebrew supply store that served beer. Kloth's belief was that homebrewers would buy a pint or two with every visit, creating multiple revenue streams.

Word of the venture reached Bruce McConnell, who wanted to be a part of it. The beer-savvy McConnell was president of the Arizona Society of Homebrewers (ASH). Before long, the three beer enthusiasts were sitting around McConnell's table discussing different business models. The Papago Brewing concept was hatched without financing or a business plan. The partners possessed no restaurant, bar or commercial brewing experience either. It was just three homebrewers driven by their love and passion for beer.

As with many visionary ideas, there were obstacles to overcome. Local zoning issues prevented them from being able to brew their own beer on-site. While the company would go on to achieve almost cult-like status with some of their Papago Brewing beers, at no point in its history did the company ever produce its own beer in house.

Since many people thought Papago was an actual brewery, Kloth and his partners had to regularly educate consumers that Papago was a brewing company, not a brewery. Other well-known brands started with the same business model of having beers contract brewed, such as Boston Beer, Schmaltz Brewing and Pete's Wicked Ale.

Being early pioneers of craft beer in the Phoenix area, one of Papago's biggest obstacles was educating the masses about beer. A small percentage of the population were homebrewers and beer geeks who were in sync with Papago's concept, but it took time to teach the masses that beer could be more than bland, yellow, fizzy liquid.

Papago regularly held beer tastings and education classes to further the understanding of this new type of beer called "craft" that was gaining popularity. The company even produced its own weekly beer newsletter to further the cause.

Another huge obstacle for this craft-centric beer destination was trying to get distributors to carry out-of-state craft beer. The partners identified, then solved, the problem by going to the extreme. Bruce McConnell left the Papago partnership to start his own beer distributorship with his son. McConnell needed to divest himself of ownership of the bar due to laws that prohibited someone from simultaneously owning a stake in a bar and a distributorship. McConnell sold his stake to his stepson, Johnny Miller, who became an active partner in the business.

The new distributorship was called Little Guy Distributing. Through Little Guy, many up-and-coming craft and international breweries finally had someone interested in bringing their brands into Arizona. Many of these brands became national powerhouses over the coming decades. Little Guy systematically put together a strong portfolio including rising stars such as Dogfish Head, Avery, Lost Abbey, Ska and world-renowned imports such as Cantillon and Van Steenberge. Crescent Crown Distributing eventually acquired Little Guy, retaining sales rep Chuck Noll, who eventually became the head of Crescent Crown's craft division.

Paul Gunn was good friends with Joe Bob Grisham, the brewer at Tempe's Bandersnatch Brewing. Gunn inquired about the possibility of Papago brewing beer on Bandersnatch's system. Grisham agreed. Since Kloth, Gunn and McConnell were all homebrewers, each of them took a homebrew recipe to Bandersnatch to brew commercially.

Kloth recalled the thought process behind what to brew:

We knew we didn't just want to make the same boring styles of beer that everyone else was making at the time, such as amber, hefeweizen, stout, and pale ale. Paul Gunn's recipe was a dark Nut Brown called Maduro Nut Brown. Bruce McConnell's recipe was called El Robusto Porter, which we considered to be a Baltic porter, though today it would probably be considered a black IPA. I brewed a Wheat Wine, a 9.6% monster of a beer, that I believe, was the strongest beer made in Arizona at the time. There were only two other places in the country that had made that style so it was pretty unique.

The process of brewing at Bandersnatch was rather cumbersome, since Bandersnatch did not have a keg cleaner. The Papago guys took kegs to a downtown Phoenix brewery named Tommyknockers, where they'd clean and sanitize them. Then they'd immediately race back to Bandersnatch in Tempe to fill the kegs while they were still clean and sanitized. Finally, they'd rush the filled kegs back to Papago's cooler before the kegs would get warm, which doesn't take long in hot Phoenix.

After about a year of this hectic practice, they contracted with Uwe Boer of what was then called Sonora Brewing. Boer handled the entirety of the process, allowing the partners to focus on their business. It was around this time that Papago wanted to focus more on being a craft beer destination and less of a homebrew shop. The homebrew supplies were eliminated, and Paul Gunn moved on to new adventures. Gunn left the business but retained his shares in the company until 2010, when he sold them to night manager Zach Ogle.

Later, when Sonoran (formerly Sonora) split into two separate companies, the brewing of Papago beers went to Sonoran Brewing's Scott Yarosh. During this period, the Papago group really hit the experimental phase of brewing different styles of beer. This is when Orange Blossom, Elsie's Coffee Milk Stout and Coconut Joe were created and distributed in kegs.

Papago sold a lot of beer from other breweries. One of the most popular was Bert Gran's Mandarin Orange from Yakima, Washington. Incidentally, Bert happened to be a frequent visitor to Papago, as he had a home in the area. After Grant's brewery went out of business, Johnny Miller suggested Papago should brew its own version of this beer style.

Kloth purchased Torani coffee syrup flavorings, and he and the Papago staff experimented with different concentrations of orange and vanilla infused into a basic wheat beer. Once a formula reached consensus, the partners decided to brew it on a larger scale. The rest is history. Orange Blossom took on a life of its own, its popularity skyrocketing, creating a demand for distribution.

The Torani syrups have been replaced with flavorings specifically designed for beer use. Papago Orange Blossom is now the no. 2 selling beer produced in the state of Arizona behind Four Peaks Kilt Lifter, quite an accomplishment for a brewing company that didn't even have its own brewery.

When quality control issues arose, Oak Creek Brewing of Sedona began brewing Papago's beers, doing so for years. Eventually Jeff Huss, husband of Papago's general manager and co-owner Leah Huss, wanted to open up his own brewery. Papago entered into a contract with Jeff to brew Papago beers upon his brewery's opening.

Huss Brewing became the first brewer to can Papago's beers. In 2016, Jeff approached Papago about buying out the brand and making it part of the Huss portfolio. It made financial sense for both sides at the time, and Papago sold its beer portfolio to Huss Brewing.

During its almost two decades of existence, Papago Brewing set the standard for what it meant to be a craft beer destination with thirty taps, two casks and about five hundred varieties of bottles/cans. When its own beers were added to the mix, it helped Papago stay ahead of the curve, even as other competition entered the market.

Papago became advocates for beers from all around the world, particularly those from Germany and Belgium. These relationships led to collaborations with some of these legendary breweries such as Van Steenberge in Belgium. The two forces collaborated to produce Papago Oude Zuipers, an 11.5% Belgian Tripel. According to Kloth, Oude Zuipers may have been the first "Arizona" beer regularly sold out of state. (It was produced in Belgium.) It was available in California and had been on tap at various times in Illinois, Colorado and Washington, D.C.

Being a leader in the Phoenix beer scene, Papago influenced so many changes in the Arizona beer scene. Besides being a force in bringing in

Papago Orange Blossom. A Phoenix mainstay. *Courtesy of Huss Brewing.*

new beers to Arizona, Papago helped write the so-called growler law that made it legal for bars to sell beer in growlers. The first draft of the bill was hammered out by Kloth and the Arizona Liquor Board in Papago's back room. Papago's significance in the region also prompted renowned German brewing powerhouse Weihenstephaner to move its U.S. sales force from Charlotte to Arizona.

Another mark of distinction was in its early years, Papago Brewing was rated as one of the twenty best places to drink beer in the *world* by RateBeer. com. According to Kloth, "I found it somewhat funny that more people out of state knew about us than in state. We started out as a beer geek place but ended up being loved by the mainstream for a totally fluky beer that turned out to be perfect for Arizona."

The folks at Papago liked to get a rise out of its loyal customers from time to time. On one particular April Fool's Day, Kloth posted on Facebook that they had just tapped a keg of Russian River's Pliny the Elder, a beer with a cult-like following that wasn't even distributed in Arizona. Within minutes, area beer lovers rushed in for this highly sought-after beer. Not actually having any Pliny, bartenders substituted Papago Hopfather instead.

Patrons raved about this legendary, rare beer, having no idea they were consuming a readily accessible imposter. When some of these beer geeks later found out they were the butt of an April Fool's joke, many were not amused and berated Papago on social media, prompting Kloth's quote, "Lighten up, it's just beer."

All good things come to an end, and eventually, it was time for last call for the legendary Scottsdale watering hole. The landlord was planning to tear down the building that housed Papago. After contemplating whether to start all over again elsewhere, the Papago brain trust decided to call it a day. Said Kloth, "It was a great run."

While Papago closed for the final time on December 2, 2017, the memories that Papago generated will last a lifetime. In a moment of introspection about the creation of Papago, Kloth said, "I think what motivated me was the feeling I got just being around other people who were as passionate about beer as I was. There was a special fellowship and kinship that was felt by all. We were also unique in that once the customers learned about beer, they shared that knowledge with other customers and life-long friendships were formed. We were like a neighborhood bar except that the regulars weren't just from the neighborhood, they regularly came from twenty or thirty miles away."

Reflecting back on memories of Papago, Kloth recalled, "Papago was unique in a lot of ways. We had three original owners who loved and knew a lot about beer. Many people that worked at Papago over the years became leading citizens in the Arizona craft beer market. We originally hired Leah Ryan as a bartender, she quickly moved up and became general manager; then we made her a partner. She married Jeff Huss who was head brewer at BJ's in Chandler. We helped them get their own place going by moving our contract brewing operations there."

Johnny Miller has his own fond memories of his days with Papago, some at the expense of his old friend Kloth:

> *Most of the years of Papago were lean. We didn't have the funds to have things professionally done in the early years so things were mostly held together with butcher's twine and a homebrewer's engineering degree. I recall temporarily fixing our ice machine with a carrot and having to empty the jukebox of change to cover our payroll checks. We weren't into it for the money. Allowing Ron all the free draft beer he can drink (under the guise of quality control) will impact the ability of any business to make a profit, but having a front row seat to witness the growth of the craft beer industry*

in the Valley, rubbing elbows with all the great people that have made it happen has been priceless.

Today, Bruce McConnell focuses on his hobby of drag racing, competing with an old truck aptly named the Orange Blossom Special. Johnny Miller is also retired, prioritizing full-time relaxation. Ron Kloth lives in Germany, the place that inspired his foray into the beer business. Meanwhile, Leah Huss has become one of the industry's leading voices and a local beer community icon. The beers once dreamed up by the Papago partners, including Leah Huss, are now owned and being brewed by the Huss family brewery, another example of things coming full circle, a testament to the tight-knit community that is the Phoenix craft beer scene.

Pedal Haus Brewery

Set aside the myth about college towns being ghost towns in the summertime. It's a hot July Monday night, and this place in the heart of Sun Devil country in Tempe is packed yet again.

In a few short years, Pedal Haus has become the destination place for beer lovers, crafting some of Arizona's finest malt beverages. Pedal Haus is the vision of Julian Wright, the Phoenix-area restaurateur and founder of Fork & Dagger Concepts. His partner in crime is brewmaster Derek "Doc" Osborne. Born in Pennsylvania, Arizona State graduate Wright is well-known locally for creating a plethora of hot spots on Mill Avenue and beyond, while the California-born Osborne has been crafting award-winning beers in the Phoenix valley for almost two decades.

Upon graduating from ASU, Wright relocated to Denver, Colorado, to become part of the Z'Teca organization, the precursor to today's popular fast-food chain Q'Doba. In eighteen short months, Wright went from assistant manager to national director of franchise operations. An opportunity within the company arose that brought Wright back as vice president of operations for the Phoenix area.

Envisioning life on the other side of corporate America, Wright left the comfort and predictability of the chain restaurant world, founding his own restaurant group with the intent to open multiple restaurant and bar concepts. He successfully opened several hot spots on Tempe's famed Mill Avenue as well as outposts in Albuquerque, New Mexico.

While in New Mexico, Wright first experienced craft beer at his Whisque Mesquite Grill and Bar when he enjoyed Marble Brewing IPA. Wright was intrigued by the beer's flavors and aromas.

After a few years in Albuquerque, Wright returned to Tempe in 2008 and opened La Bocca Pizzeria and Wine Bar, a spot that enjoys critical acclaim to this day. He continued his enthusiasm for local craft by carrying Arizona-brewed beers at all his locations, long before it was en vogue. Hop Knot and Kilt Lifter, from the popular Tempe-based Four Peaks Brewing Company, became staples on his list.

Wright continued to open hot spots in the heart of Arizona State's Mill Avenue, as the area possessed the urban core feel that resonated with Wright. He was slowly but surely building a hospitality empire on the campus of his alma mater.

The local craft beer scene was growing, as was Wright's interest in it. This enthusiasm led to the opening of his bicycle-themed modern American beer garden called Handlebar Tempe in 2012. Handlebar featured twenty-four taps and delivered a plethora of craft beer options. Wright homed in on the exploding craft scene, turning Handlebar into one of the city's go-to places for new and rare craft beers.

Wright began to travel internationally and had the opportunity to spend some time in Belgium, considered to be the holy grail for beer lovers. During his travels, he re-envisioned an earlier idea that hadn't yet come to fruition— opening a place that produced its own beer. Originally hatched as an idea to brew beer exclusively for Handlebar, the vision expanded quickly to become a full-scale brewpub where patrons could enjoy a great meal paired with beers produced on-site. Planning began in earnest.

Remaining in his comfort zone of Mill Avenue, Wright was searching for a modest location when he discovered a cavernous space at 730 South Mill Avenue with eight thousand square feet inside and another six thousand outside. Wright originally dismissed the parcel as nonviable. However, the high ceilings and tree-lined streets did appeal to Wright, and because it was set back off the main drag of Mill, the rent was less expensive.

Wanting to build a European-style bistro and brewery, Wright went for it, signing a lease in 2015 that locked in the property for thirty years. He sold his other properties to focus on his new concept. All in, he had to figure out how to build a brewpub and determine who would brew the beers that would make or break this new concept.

A mutual friend introduced Wright to a local brewing legend named Derek "Doc" Osborne. Wright requested a consultative meeting with Osborne for

Inside the spacious Pedal Haus Brewery. *Courtesy of Pedal Haus.*

advice on building a brewery, something Osborne had plenty of experience with working at BJ's Brewhouse. Wright presented his ideas and overall vision. Taking his consulting role seriously, Osborne viewed Wright's project as if he were designing his *own* brewhouse.

Wright recalls the early interactions with his future partner Osborne. "I didn't know anything about opening a brewery. When I was introduced to Doc, he was always willing to lend a hand, advising me all the while," said Wright.

The two met again about a week later, as Wright had more questions. During that second meeting, Wright mentioned how he was in the market for a brewer. "While I thought he might be interested in being my partner, when it came down to it, he turned me down. He said he was comfortable where he was at currently. I was disappointed," Wright recalled.

Undeterred, Wright knew that this brewery-in-planning had the potential to develop into something special. Because of the tight-knit relationship he had developed rather quickly with Osborne, he knew he'd make a great partner. Wright asked Osborne for one more meeting. This time, he encouraged Osborne to bring his wife, Melissa, a fellow professional brewer at Four Peaks Brewery.

The three met and got along great, prompting Wright to make a competitive offer to Osborne to become the brewmaster and minority partner. As Osborne contemplated the offer, Melissa received reassurance from the partners at Four Peaks who knew Wright well and vouched for his character as a person and a businessman. That assurance helped ease trepidation from the Osbornes. Wright's loyalty to Four Peaks all those years was repaid with this act of good karma.

While Osborne was completely satisfied working for BJ's, the magnetic pull of partial brewery ownership was too much to pass up. Seeing ownership as the only way to progress any further in the industry, Osborne agreed to join forces with Wright to start Pedal Haus together. The name Pedal Haus continued the bicycle theme Wright created when he founded his popular Handlebar.

"Growing up in Canada, we biked everywhere as a family," said Wright. "That tradition carried on during my time at ASU."

Osborne stayed on at BJ's for about four months, to ensure a smooth transition. Once Pedal Haus received the OK to commence brewing operations, Osborne left BJ's and began his new brewing chapter as the head of brewing operations for Pedal Haus.

After assembling the brewhouse and coming up with some initial recipes, one of his first orders of business was to hire an able assistant brewer. That turned out to be the affable Ian Campbell-O'Neill, who was brewing at a neighboring Tempe brewery, Blasted Barley, at the time. The two made a great team, producing some of the highest-quality beers anywhere in Arizona.

Making effective use of this huge space was a daunting challenge. They had to take some chances and big leaps. Some ideas worked flawlessly, while others did not. When all was said and done, the brewpub became the jewel of Mill Avenue, propelling Pedal Haus into the conversation of best Phoenix breweries. For all its momentum, a fair share of challenges remained.

As Wright recalled, "We opened with a Belgian restaurant and beer theme but with a different décor and vibe than we have now. It was working, but we were struggling with type of food that we committed to serving. It was much more high-end than a typical brewery."

The beer lineup featured old-world classics from Belgium and Germany, such as saison, dubbel, wit, pilsner and dortmunder, which were all well received. Curiously, the team decided not to brew their own IPA, the de facto no. 1 craft beer style in America. Instead, Wright's original plan was to satisfy the hop crowd by bringing in guest IPAs. It was a missed opportunity.

Kölsch   Blanche   IPA   Porter

Above: Pedal Haus sampler.

Left: Bourbon barrel-aged stout from Pedal Haus. *Courtesy of Pedal Haus.*

When Pedal Haus opened, it also served mass-produced beers such as Coors Light. The owners did so because they were located on a college campus, and that's what college kids requested. However, a brewery's true profit margins come from selling its own beer. Between the Belgian food theme, the interesting beer choices and space usage issues, there were a few disconnects for the Pedal Haus team to correct.

Although many would argue Pedal Haus may have already been the most impressive brewpub in Arizona at the time, Wright decided that what he envisioned and what he created were not the same. Just one year into operation, Pedal Haus decided to undergo a significant redesign to better appeal to its clientele while showcasing the brewery in a much more prominent way. Wright noted,

> We are in a tourist heavy, event-driven area, so we needed to have food you can get out of the kitchen quickly. Unintentionally, my naivety was not putting enough emphasis on the brewery, since I came from a restaurant background. I came to realize the beer is the star and everything else should enhance that. I had remorse that my space didn't feel enough like a brewery. Then I thought, let's pivot, and be a brewery with great food instead of a restaurant that makes its own beer.

After the remodel, Pedal Haus reopened and was an instant hit. Saturday night or Monday afternoon, the place was always abuzz. It didn't take long for Pedal Haus to become the talk of the Arizona brewing scene. That popularity was enhanced when Wright relented and agreed to let Osborne brew an IPA, making the place even more popular. Checking in at 6.5% ABV and only 53 IBU, the IPA immediately became the brewery's no. 1 seller.

The first beer Osborne and his team won an award for was at the Los Angeles International Beer Competition for the German-style Dortmunder Lager. "That is, by far, my favorite beer style and my favorite beer Doc has ever made," said Wright. "If I could only have one beer in the world, that's the one I would choose. Not many people make that beer style. It was a thrill for me winning an award for that beer; it was a milestone, and it put us on the map."

Another milestone came in the sale of the first keg to an off-site account. While most of the beer is produced to sell in-house, the first keg distributed, the IPA, was sold to the Grind in Arcadia. Around the same time, they began to rethink the whole "Coors Light" thing. The brain trust began to wonder if it was wise selling a lot of beer produced by another brewery when Osborne was more than capable of producing something similar. Sales of Coors Light were quite high, and it took a leap of faith to discontinue carrying the brand.

Osborne created a delicious and refreshing Light Lager, yellow-straw in color, checking in under 4.0% ABV. Brewed for the first time in the spring of 2017, Light Lager quickly became Pedal Haus' no. 2 beer and won several awards. It was the gold medal winner at the 2017 LA International Beer Competition and won a bronze in the same competition the following year. It earned a gold at the North American Beer Awards and won its most prestigious medal, a silver, at the Great American Beer Festival in 2017.

The third-most popular beer in the lineup is the first beer ever brewed at Pedal Haus, Bière Blanche. A Belgian Wit beer in the spirit of Wright's original vision for the company, Bière Blanche was the best-of-show winner at the Arizona Brewer's Bowl in 2017.

Tragically, Osborne's trusted right-hand man, twenty-seven-year-old Ian Campbell-O'Neill, was killed in a motorcycle accident in March 2017. It was a shock not only for the Pedal Haus family but also to the entire brewing community of Arizona. Campbell-O'Neill left a positive impression on everyone he met, making his loss so heartbreaking for the entire community.

Osborne cited the community coming together after Ian's passing as the most memorable event in the history of Pedal Haus Brewery. The brewery held a fundraiser on his behalf that brought a full house of over six hundred mourning friends who shared beers and celebrated the life of Campbell-O'Neill.

As a tribute to Campbell-O'Neill, the brewery produced a hazy, rye-based IPA called RiCon. It stood for Rye Ian Campbell-O'Neill, named before it was even released. One of Ian's favorite breweries was Modern Times of San Diego, California. Wright recalled, "When the people at Modern Times heard about Ian's death, they reached out to us. They offered to brew a collaboration beer in his honor. It was an amazing gesture. As a two-year-old brewery in Tempe to be recognized by a brewery with a stature of Modern Times, it reinforced the collaborative nature of the beer industry. The support and generosity within our industry just blew me away," said Wright.

Osborne handled brewing duties solely for an extended period of time. Eventually, Ian's position needed to be filled, and serendipitously, the position was filled by Campbell-O'Neill's former roommate Ben Love. While Campbell-O'Neill will never be forgotten, the new dynamic duo continues to produce award-winning beers as good as any in the Phoenix market and beyond.

Looking back on the success he's achieved in the restaurant business and, specifically, at Pedal Haus, Wright waxed philosophical: "There's been times when I wanted to give up. But it's all about continuing to grow and evolve. Sometimes the things that are the hardest are the most rewarding. This journey we've been on, designing the space, creating the menu, and the incredible beer; it has been such a positive experience. It's truly a living, breathing thing. Pedal Haus is not about one person, it's a collection of people working hard, side by side, getting it to evolve to be the best it can be."

SanTan Brewing Company

The original SanTan Brewing Company location opened in 2007 in historic downtown Chandler, founded by former Four Peaks brewer Anthony Canecchia and his partners, with a goal of pairing craft beer with craft food over great conversation.

It is a popular full-service brewpub, and patrons come for the food as readily as for the beer. The beers of SanTan Brewing have created quite a following. Winning multiple high-profile awards didn't hurt, including medaling at the following events: 2011 Great American Beer Festival, 2012 US Open Beer Championships and 2016 World Beer Cup, among others.

A local Arizona leader when it comes to innovation, SanTan canned its beers long before it became mainstream. Canning helped establish SanTan as a leader in its field. Rallying around this concept led to SanTan hosting an annual event known as AmeriCan, a beer festival centered on breweries that embrace canning, a practice that has now become widespread among breweries both local and nationwide.

When demand outpaced what the taxed brewpub brewery could handle, a full-scale production facility was opened a few miles from the brewpub that handled the production of beers for distribution. The brewpub continued to make beer that was served within its walls.

Besides AmeriCan, SanTan hosts an annual Oktoberfest celebration that brings thousands of people to downtown Chandler for a day and evening of fun, food and, naturally, beer.

In December 2017, SanTan announced its plans to open a second brewpub location in Uptown Phoenix at Bethany Station, expanding its footprint.

Its flagship Devil's Ale, an American pale ale, 5.5% ABV, 45 IBU, features Cascade, Centennial and Simcoe hops that deliver a piney/citrus aromatic experience. This beer pairs well with pizza and pulled pork. MoonJuice Galactic IPA checks in at 7.3% ABV, 65 IBU, featuring the highly sought-after Southern Hemisphere hops of Galaxy and Nelson Sauvin. Tropical fruit aromas and flavors abound from these prized hops.

Mr. Pineapple, a beer that was originally intended to be a one-off for an upcoming outdoor event, has blossomed into an Arizona favorite. 5% ABV, 15 IBU, this easy-drinking wheat ale made with real pineapple juice is just what the hot, dry temperatures of Arizona call for, especially in the heart of the summer.

SanTan's brewery has nurtured a great deal of brewing talent within its walls, starting or advancing many Arizona brewers' careers, including Patrick Ware, Chase Saraiva and Nick Pauley (Arizona Wilderness), Jesse Kortepeter (Wanderlust, Oro) and Josh Telich (McFate), to name a few.

SanTan Brewing Company celebrated its tenth anniversary in September 2017. Operating under the mantra "Arizona Owned, Arizona Brewed," SanTan embraces its southwest roots and is proud to be Arizona's second-largest producer of beer behind Four Peaks Brewing Company and the largest Arizona-owned brewery.

Scottsdale Beer Company

What do you get when you put two restaurant lifers together who share a love for great beer? You get a first-rate brewpub.

Scottsdale Beer Company is the brainchild of Doug Ledger and Tom Davidson. Equal parts opportunists and entrepreneurs, the partners observed a lack of quality brewpubs when they hatched their idea to open Scottsdale Beer Company in 2011. At the time, the city had just one brewpub, and they knew Scottsdale craved more.

Davidson started down a craft beer path working for Pyramid Breweries in Seattle, Washington, for almost a decade. Incidentally, he worked for George Hancock, who would later go on to leave his own legacy in the Phoenix brewing scene. Davidson handled mostly front-of-house duties for Pyramid while concurrently developing a palate for fine beers. Davidson moved to Phoenix in 2006 and immediately immersed himself in the local Scottsdale restaurant industry.

Doug Ledger is originally from Fort Collins, Colorado, a town rich in craft-brewing tradition. Living just minutes from craft beer powerhouses New Belgium and Odell's, Ledger grew up on craft beer. "We went to breweries instead of bars," Ledger said. He, too, moved to the Phoenix area, beating his future partner to Arizona by eight months. Although they both worked in the restaurant industry, the two eventually met through a mutual friend on a golf course, hitting it off immediately.

As the friendship developed, they philosophized on what it took to create a true destination place. Both believed the pillars of success were grounded in three basic concepts: great food, a solid beer list and excellent service.

At the time, Arizona was behind the curve when it came to craft brewing. Despite being the nation's sixth-largest state, Arizona had fewer breweries than San Diego County alone. The partners saw vast opportunity in Arizona, especially in the underserved brewpub arena.

Deep down, Davidson always knew he was interested in opening his own restaurant. Working for a local brewpub, Davidson was keenly aware of the brewpub's popularity. Witnessing this firsthand strengthened his resolve to open a place of his own. It was time to have a serious talk with his old friend Doug Ledger.

The two shared many of the same ideas, as well as similar passions. They decided to go for it and open a brewpub. A brewpub built on their pillars for success would fill the market need they identified earlier. They respected independent operations that beat to their own drum, and the two intended to do the same.

Searching for real estate for about a year, they viewed fifty-three different sites that traversed the entire Metro Phoenix area. They kept coming back to the third site they visited at the intersection of the 101 and Shea Boulevard in Scottsdale because it had most of what they were seeking. A former restaurant site, it had the proper square footage needed and a willingness from the landlord to allow extensive build-outs needed to accommodate a brewery.

It wasn't as easy as signing a lease, however. Due to issues with the previous tenant, each of the neighboring businesses had clauses in their contracts that enabled them to have influence, or reject outright, any potential tenant that might negatively affect their business. It took about eight months to satisfy the neighboring businesses and move forward.

Reconstruction began and took seven grueling months. Ledger and Davidson persevered, did a lot of the work themselves and filled twenty-two dumpsters gutting the contents of the former tenant.

All the while they were constructing their new business, they had the ever-looming challenge of dealing with the federal government to acquire their brewer's license. True to form, the government made them work for it. It

Exterior of Scottsdale Beer Company. *Courtesy of SBC.*

took a full twelve months between the time they started the process until the time they received their license allowing them to brew.

Through Tom's wife, they met a homebrewer interested in moving to the professional level. Being seasoned veterans in the restaurant industry, neither Ledger nor Davidson had any plans to hire a homebrewer. With so much on the line, they intended to hire a seasoned, experienced professional.

As a courtesy to Tom's wife, Davidson agreed to meet with homebrewer Brad Williams. The two met at a local Whole Foods store. With no serious intent of considering Williams for the position due to his inexperience, Davidson told Ledger to call him one hour into the meeting with a prefabricated "emergency" to allow him to exit the meeting gracefully. What Davidson didn't anticipate was the immediate bond he made with Williams. When the conversation finally ended three hours later, Davidson knew he had found his brewer. He took a chance on the "rookie," and Williams has been the company's head brewer ever since.

Consulting with industry veterans, including Eric Walter (Dogfish Head) and George Hancock (Pyramid, Phoenix Ale Brewery), the team began to build their brewhouse and construct their restaurant. While the physical construction was underway, they concurrently worked on the food and beer menus. When the brewing system arrived from Germany, it came with an engineer who spent three weeks teaching Williams the nuances of operating the equipment properly. Whatever Williams may not have known going into the position, he learned during that intense three weeks of training.

Before joining the team, Williams had a lucrative job with great benefits. He had a wife and a mortgage, but like the partners, he took his own leap of faith to realize a lifelong dream of becoming a professional brewer. It paid off for Williams, as he became a limited partner a few years later after continuously exceeding expectations.

Scottsdale Beer Company (SBC) became the state of Arizona's sixty-second brewery when it opened on New Year's Eve, December 21, 2014. The team was immediately put to the test with a full house, a test they aced.

Shortly thereafter, it was time for SBC to enter its first professional contest, the Arizona Strong Beer Festival competition. SBC came away with two medals. Competing for the first time at the Great American Beer Festival in 2017, arguably the world's most prestigious beer competition, SBC won a bronze medal for its Cannonball international pale ale.

The beers crafted at Scottsdale Beer Company appeal both to the casual consumer and the educated beer aficionado. East End Amber is a slightly malt-forward red ale with beautiful clarity and a lasting, off-white head. The clean-finishing beer pairs great with chicken, burgers and pepperoni pizza.

The German-style Hefeweizen is true to the Bavarian style. With flavors and aromas of banana and clove on a soft backbone of wheat, Hefeweizen is light and refreshing.

Downshift Session IPA is packed with fruity citrus hop aroma and flavor that appropriately dominate this IPA. Gold and clear, the beer is light bodied and palate cleansing. Downshift is a great pairing with anything deep fried, especially the extremely popular walleye dinner.

Tom's wife ended up with a beer curiously named in her honor with Big Mouth Blonde, the brewery's no. 1 seller. This was in tribute to her making the connection to Williams, the man they eventually hired as their head brewer.

One of Williams's favorite beers to brew is his popular Texas Tea. This double-chocolate stout may look like crude oil but has flavors that span the spectrum. Cocoa nibs, vanilla and chocolate all contribute flavors and aromas before it is aged in whiskey barrels to give it additional complexity and character. Williams has crafted various iterations of the beer over the years, including one with ancho chiles, serrano peppers and jalapeños, showcasing the beer's southwestern heritage.

View from the Scottsdale Beer Company brewhouse. *Courtesy of SBC.*

Head chef Justin Olsen worked for highly acclaimed Phoenix chef Kevin Binkley for five years honing his skills. Collaborating with Williams, the two intertwine flavors of the beers into many of the menu items. A clear synergy exists between the kitchen and the brewery.

The company began distributing beer locally in September 2017. The team did their due diligence, talking with local distributors for over six months until choosing Quail Distributing to be their distributor.

"We were on the same page with them," said Ledger. "They had good strategies and we decided it was the right fit for us. So far, our beer has been exceeding their expectations," he said.

Part of Scottsdale Beer Company's success lies in its connection to the community. Every year, the company holds a fundraiser known as "shop with a cop." In 2017, SBC raised enough money for 340 underprivileged kids to enjoy a Christmas that would not otherwise have been possible. Each child was accompanied by an officer, firefighter or military member to a local store, where they received a $100 gift card to spend on themselves.

Another charitable initiative is SBC's work with Cortney's Place, a center that assists adults with intellectual and developmental disabilities. SBC has raised over $100,000 in the past three years for this organization. Families involved with Cortney's Place pay nothing for its services. The brewery raises

10 percent of the charity's annual budget in one evening of fundraising each year, a testament to the connection the brewery has with the local community.

Years working in the industry gave Ledger and Davidson the vision to create their ideal business. Their mantra of great food and service paired with outstanding beer has come to life in the form of Scottsdale Beer Company. Mission accomplished.

The Shop Beer Company

Dave Arnce, Dylan DeMiguel and Jason Calhoon, the three amigos behind The Shop Beer Company, put a lot of thought into tying a name to their identity. Proposing hundreds of names that just didn't resonate, they wanted to come up with a "feel good" name that would be relatable to anyone, anywhere.

The under construction, yet unnamed brewery, was affectionately known as "the shop" in casual conversation. Referring to this space as *the shop* became almost second nature. Eventually, the partners agreed to adopt it as the brewery's official moniker. This, however, isn't the start of the story. The story starts over coffee.

Dave Arnce, the founder and creative director of The Shop Beer Company, went to ASU, where he studied human nutrition and biochemistry. After college, Arnce briefly relocated to California before returning to Phoenix to start a real estate finance company. The company did well, enabling him to sell the business and focus on his long-held passion of being in a people-centric industry. The creative and driven Arnce invested his time in projects that satisfied that passion. Owning a brewery was at the top of that list.

Becoming involved with Cartel Coffee Company as it looked to expand its offerings beyond coffee, Arnce envisioned creating a company specializing in hand-crafted beverages pairing Cartel Brewery and Cartel Coffee under one roof. It was here that a partnership was formed.

The trio that would later found The Shop Beer Company act like a family because they are family. Dylan DeMiguel, director of sales and marketing, is Dave's brother-in-law. Married to Dylan's sister Mikel Anne, he has been best friends with Dylan since they met. While Dylan was in college, the two daydreamed about owing a business together. Little did they know an opportunity was right around the corner.

Jason Calhoon worked in retail for most of his life, with varied work experiences including a background in specialty coffee. He found a niche

Left to right: Dave Arnce, Jason Calhoun and Dylan DeMiguel of The Shop Beer Company. *Courtesy of The Shop Beer Company.*

inbrewing operations when Arnce first launched the original Cartel Brewery operation. His passion for brewing expanded from there.

DeMiguel explained the drive behind Arnce wanting to be a brewery owner: "Dave started homebrewing in college and found something magnetic about it. He found that brewing had aspects of community and culture, and that the beer industry is the perfect balance of art and science."

Eventually, it was mutually decided among the Cartel leadership team to focus separately on coffee and beer. This new direction led to the birth of a new company. Led by Arnce, the trio set out to create a new brand with a whole new identity. The Shop Beer Company was born.

Dealing with the typical brewery building delays from construction to government approvals, it took twenty months to get The Shop Beer Company open. The partners built a twenty-barrel brewhouse, putting their energy and finances on the line. Deciding to go big or go home, they bet on the booming craft beer market, their connections and themselves. The Shop Beer Company opened in August 2016. Reinvesting in themselves, the partners effectively increased its fermentation space by 300 percent in just nine months.

DeMiguel handles all sales, marketing and distribution. Calhoon is in charge of brewing operations, while Arnce runs the overall business, including financials and purchasing. With his chemistry background, Arnce co-creates the recipes with Calhoon.

In February 2017, The Shop Beer Company signed an agreement with Hensley Distributing to distribute its beers statewide. Attacking the draft market, The Shop Beer Company built its brand one keg at a time, seeking accounts that understand the emerging local craft beer scene. Limited canning produces additional opportunities to enjoy The Shop's beers.

"The best part about craft beer is the exploration," says DeMiguel. "If people are talking about The Shop Beer Company, chances are they are talking about the creativity of the beers," he said.

Church Music is a "juicy" IPA, checking in at 6.7% ABV, 46 IBU. A relatively new take on a classic beer style, this beer showcases the hop flavor, especially the hops-derived pineapple notes. Church Music is the brewery's best-seller in the taproom and in distribution.

F.Y.I.T.M. (pronounced "Fight 'em") is an acronym for Five Years In The Making. This West Coast–style double IPA packs a sneaky punch at 10.1% ABV, 107 IBU. Traditional West Coast IPA characteristics lead, with a crisp bitterness and tons of hop aroma.

Coffee Brown brings the partners' two worlds together in one delicious beer. This 6.6% ABV, 31 IBU American Nut Brown ale is brewed with coffee. An ode to their coffee-making roots, this beer is available on both CO_2 and nitro. Using a combination of cold brew and ground whole beans, the unique flavor profile has a subtle nut flavor with a smooth hint of coffee. F.Y.I.T.M. and Coffee Brown are popular Shop beers that have been carried over from the days of Cartel Brewing. Food trucks supply patrons with unique cuisine while beer-to-go is available in crowlers, growlers and assorted cans.

The tasting room is located in a historic house built in the 1950s that was previously home to Harry Mitchell and his son Mark, former and current mayors of Tempe. They paid careful attention to restore the house to its previous glory, and the bar is found inside, with a spacious beer garden separating the taproom from the 3,200-square-foot brewery.

"Our guests can feel the brand by visiting the tasting room," said DeMiguel. "Customers can look directly into the brewery, giving them the ability to see the action of beer making in progress."

With its comfortable location, The Shop Beer Company makes people feel like they are at a neighborhood block party. Open seven days a week, there's no better way to party than with good friends and great beers.

Uncle Bear's

Bear was more than man's best friend. He was the inspiration behind Todd Carey's Uncle Bear's Grill and Tap restaurant concept that opened back in the summer of 2000. A black lab mix, Bear was a rescue dog that became Carey's travel companion as he traversed the Southwest in what doubled as his personal beer discovery journey. Bear's presence is felt in every Uncle Bear's location, each providing a fun atmosphere where friends and family can enjoy a variety of delicious menu selections as well as its fresh, locally brewed beer. With a mantra of "Come, Sit and Stay," Uncle Bear's is a place where everyone, including the family pet, is welcome.

The first Uncle Bear's restaurant was established in 2000 in Gilbert, Arizona. A restaurant without a brewery, it spawned other locations in Mesa, Queen Creek, Chandler and Surprise. In 2013, due to his growing passion for craft beer, owner Todd Carey decided to enhance the concept and open his first brewpub, a restaurant with an onsite brewery. Being inspired by some of the great beers of California, he wanted to bring similar flavors and styles to the Arizona desert. The brewpub opened in the east valley neighborhood of Ahwatukee.

The original plan was to brew beer solely for the Uncle Bear's restaurant locations, with no distribution. That concept was immediately challenged with multiple inquiries to purchase Uncle Bear's beer.

At first, kegs were self-distributed in the market, which created long workdays for the brewery staff and one-man sales team. As distribution grew, Uncle Bear's partnered with Young's Market to distribute the beers, providing a statewide reach. This allowed the brewers to focus on what they did best, brew beer.

In 2016, the brewery started to can, opening new retail markets. Initially, two core beers were canned. Mandarin's Best Friend, an easy-drinking 5.1% ABV, 12 IBU mandarin orange wheat beer, and Ocean Beach West Coast "Style" IPA, a personal favorite of Carey. 6.9% ABV and 60 IBU, Ocean Beach is brewed with generous hop additions that provide citrus and floral aromas and flavors.

Barkley's Peanut Butter Cup Porter (5.4% ABV and 20 IBU) became the third canned beer in 2017. Barkley's is a dark and decadent American-style porter that is made with real peanut butter cups, balancing flavors of chocolate and peanut butter. In 2018, Fence Jumper Golden Ale (4.8% ABV, 15 IBU) and Wolfhound Irish Red Ale (4.6% ABV, 19 IBU) were added to the canning lineup.

Todd Carey, founder, Uncle Bear's. *Courtesy of Uncle Bear's.*

Uncle Bear's taproom. *Courtesy of Uncle Bear's.*

With demand growing at a brisk pace, Carey took the plunge and opened an eighteen-thousand-square-foot production brewing facility in Gilbert in October 2018. It was a bit of a homecoming returning to the town where the very first Uncle Bear's location opened almost two decades earlier. This facility produces all Uncle Bear's beers, making production in Ahwatukee no longer necessary.

An on-site taproom and yard allow patrons to enjoy freshly made beers just steps from where they're brewed, providing an interactive experience. Patrons witness brewing activities while playing games, listening to live music or nibbling on tasty grub from a visiting food truck.

A consistent canine and beach vibe exists at all Uncle Bear's locations, whether it's the Grill & Tap hot spots in Ahwatukee, Mesa and Queen Creek or the new brewery/taproom in Gilbert. People may come for the comfortable vibe, but they sit, and stay, for the beer. Bear would be very proud.

WEST VALLEY BREWERIES

8-Bit Aleworks

8-Bit Aleworks is an unobtrusive, Avondale microbrewery built by owners Ryan and Krystina Whitten to celebrate two of their favorite things: gaming and craft beer. 8-Bit's distinctive retro gaming theme is woven into every element of the brewery, from the tasting room ambiance to the beer names. Stepping into the tasting room, you'll experience walls decorated with hand-painted 8- and 16-bit images.

Though both are gamers, the Whittens are the first to admit that owning a brewery was never part of their original plan. Ryan earned a degree in visual effects, while Krystina holds a master's degree in forensic psychology. However, after nearly ten years homebrewing and a few successful wins in brewing competitions, Ryan realized that he had a passion for sharing good beer with others. Despite being adamant that brewing was just a hobby, it wasn't long until he realized he wanted to step into craft beer as a full-time profession.

The Whittens decided to move forward, putting all their efforts and life savings into the project. The two mapped out a plan and decided to build their brewery entirely on their own, without loans or investors. When it came to naming the brewery, 8-Bit seemed the perfect fit.

Ryan, an Avondale native, was set on building his brewery in his hometown. The City of Avondale was supportive, even eager, and became an important ally throughout the development and construction of the brewery. Between the support of the city government and being part of the local community, operating in Avondale became a rallying cry and a point of pride for the Whittens.

Even with the city on their side, opening wasn't an easy road. In order to remain self-funded, Ryan had to get very creative when designing the brewery. He engineered a keg washer and the original cooling system for the three-barrel fermenters employed at opening. He worked four jobs concurrently, and Krystina worked two, to help build capital.

Construction took longer than planned, and opening was delayed by six months. There were challenges acquiring and setting up the brew system. Despite all these obstacles, Ryan brewed his first official 8-Bit Aleworks beer in April 2015, and the couple opened their doors the next month. They spent their wedding anniversary hosting a soft opening and then opened to the public on Ryan's birthday a few days later.

8-Bit has earned a reputation for developing unique, creative brews. Some of the most intriguing beers Ryan has created include a double black IPA with Thai chiles, coconut and lime leaves; a salted chocolate gose; a

Gaming is all the rage at Avondale's 8-Bit Brewing. *Courtesy of 8-Bit Aleworks.*

boysenberry cobbler beer; a garlic gose and the brewery's flagship witbier known as White Mage.

In creating a consistent theme, the beer's names, and sometimes even the recipes, often reference games. White Mage was named and brewed in homage to the healing character from the game Final Fantasy. The recipe includes white cacao nibs and grains of paradise, considered by many to be healing ingredients.

Other game references include Hopsassin's Creed, 8-Bit's take on the Assassin's Creed game, and Legend of Zymur, a beer-related twist on the Legend of Zelda, incorporating the concept of zymurgy, the study of fermentation.

At the time of this writing, Krystina still works a full-time job outside the brewery, while Ryan handles duties at the brewery. The two partners run the majority of the business with a limited staff and have grown significantly since opening. The three-barrel plastic fermenters they had at the start have been replaced by seven-barrel stainless fermenters, more than doubling the capacity for brewing. 8-bit now does small-batch canning. The brewery's anniversary event, Final Anniversary (a Final Fantasy reference), occurs every April, with attendance surpassing five hundred people.

The Whittens hope to continue their growth at a modest pace in order to ensure quality. 8-Bit Aleworks is a place to embrace a gamer's or beer lover's inner geek and enjoy a sense of community and togetherness with some great brews.

Peoria Artisan Brewery

The seed for Peoria Artisan Brewery was planted when a friend invited Matthew Frosch to homebrew. In search of a business startup idea, Frosch knew it was time to become his own boss. That afternoon of homebrewing ignited the idea that brewing might be the answer he was seeking.

With a wife, three young daughters and no experience in the field, the idea of opening a brewery was quite a leap of faith. "My wife Kristina's initial thought was that we were crazy to consider opening our own business, especially with no real-world restaurant experience on our résumés," said Frosch. However, logic often loses out to passion.

"I have a passion for creating something from the ground up; for delivering a product and an experience to people. The brewing industry satisfies that passion. The camaraderie found in the craft beer industry also inspires me daily," said Frosch.

Matt and Kris Frosch of Peoria Artisan Brewing. *Courtesy of Kris Frosch.*

Frosch carefully composed a business plan that took years to complete. Intent on self-funding the project, the couple contributed their life savings to get the business going.

Forced to start small, the couple devised a foodless brewery/taproom concept. Knowing and accepting the challenges that lay ahead, the brewery was designed with a tiny one-barrel brewing system, capable of yielding only thirty gallons of beer per batch. Unable to find the right location at a reasonable price near their Peoria home, the Froschs signed a lease in September 2013, acquiring a cozy space in Litchfield Park. The Peoria Artisan Taproom opened for business three months later, warmly welcomed by the local community.

Still envisioning owning a brewery that served its own food, the Froschs revisited their original plan of opening a brewpub. The couple planned, budgeted and eventually opened the Peoria Artisan Brewery in November 2015, a full-service brewpub located in their hometown of Peoria. The core team of Matthew, Kristina and partner/chef Michael Mahalick run the Peoria location.

Having been with the organization from day one, Chef Michael "has become an extended member of the Frosch family as well as a partner in the business," according to Frosch. Peoria Artisan Brewery has a full kitchen and a five-barrel brewery, capable of producing ten kegs of beer per batch.

After running a brewery/taproom, adjusting to life as a full-service brewpub was eye opening. "The combination of food and food service along with brewing and beer management was quite an adjustment," said Frosch. "We've learned from others who have been successful in the industry and we now understand the importance of cost controls and budgeting." Frosch credits the experience and know-how of Mahalick as a huge factor to their successes. "Chef Michael is instrumental in maintaining our costs so we can maintain positive net revenues," he confirmed.

In May 2018, the *Arizona Republic* named Peoria Artisan as having one of the "25 best burgers in the Valley." In October 2018, it was recognized as being one of the 10 best restaurants in Peoria by AZCentral.com.

When it comes to the beers, the best-seller is Savannah Marie IPA, a 7.5% ABV, West Coast–style IPA named after the Frosch's second daughter. Light drinking 4.5% ABV Push Mower Blonde Ale is another popular offering. Peoria Artisan's Belgian Tripel, Third Sabbath, took gold in the Belgian/ Trappist category at the Arizona Strong Beer Festival in 2017.

Not able to give both locations the attention needed to truly thrive, the couple made the difficult decision to sell the taproom in 2018. "It was a tough decision for Kristina and I to sell the taproom, but we were able to sell to another team that is looking to start their own brewery. It was really a win-win for them, us and the community as we get another brewery in the West Valley," said Frosch. "The sale also allows us to reinvest and focus our efforts on our flagship location in Peoria in order to stay relevant in an increasingly competitive market."

Frosch waxes philosophical on owning a brewpub. "We have a different beer culture in the northwest valley," said Frosch. "We are family oriented and brew traditional, true-to-style beers. I think what makes us unique is how everything we do is a reflection of our customers."

Richter Aleworks

"I was never a big alcohol drinker," said the future brewery owner, Brandon Richter. Co-founder with his wife April of the eponymously named brewery, Richter Aleworks, Richter set out on an unlikely course to brewery ownership. Being inspired after watching a travel show, the couple embarked on a trip to Europe. The trip had no specific intent other than to experience new adventures.

Choosing London as their destination, the Richters and another couple made their way into a series of English pubs. While they weren't regular consumers of alcohol, the beer scene was just different in London. The seed was planted, and Brandon couldn't wait to explore and learn all he could about beer.

Deciding to make European travel an annual event, they traveled the following year to Germany. Considered by many to be the epicenter of great beer, Munich and its various ales and lagers captivated Richter. From that point forward, Richter was all-in when it came to beer.

Immediately upon returning stateside, he began homebrewing and even started a beer club to bring together passionate, like-minded beer connoisseurs. He wanted to learn everything he could about beer.

At the time, Brandon was working in the graphics industry, doing large-format printing and car wrapping, while moonlighting in real estate. April was in the mortgage business. The crash of 2007 cast doubts in their minds about a long-term career in the real estate industry.

After the following year's travels took the group to Belgium, it was settled. Being in the beer business was something Richter just had to do. Having a unique opportunity to meet and converse with Sam Calagione, founder and CEO of Delaware's Dogfish Head Brewing Company, an inspired Richter took his quest up a notch and began to look for a location to house his dream brewery. "Meeting Sam took me out of the fandom moment and made me realize this is something I can do," said Brandon.

Richter found brewing schools were booked over a year in advance. With luck on his side, Siebel Brewing Academy had a spot available, and Richter jumped at the chance and furthered his learning.

Brandon escaped the stress of his daily work life by listening to brewing podcasts, propelling his beer learning. One podcast mentioned a course that taught prospective brewery owners how to open and operate a brewery. The course took place at Colorado Boy Brewery in Ridgway, Colorado, conducted by a skilled, experienced brewery owner and entrepreneur named Tom Hennessey.

Brandon knew that making that call would officially put the plan in motion. Was he ready yet? Was he sure this was his path? On one particularly stressful March workday, Brandon picked up the phone and made the call. Hennessey himself answered and booked Brandon for a course that November.

Derek, April and Brandon Richter of Richter Aleworks. *Courtesy of Richter Aleworks.*

Continuing the path toward brewery ownership, the Richters attended that year's Craft Brewers Conference in San Diego, California. The Richters spent five days there, met all the industry rock stars and took in fourteen or fifteen breweries during the trip for learning, inspiration and contacts. Reality set in on the difficulty of starting a brewery, but the Richters persevered.

Being west-siders, the Richters recognized the dearth of breweries in Phoenix's west valley. They became determined to open in their hometown of Peoria. Peoria didn't have much experience working with prospective breweries, making the process very challenging.

Being a brand-new, unestablished entity made it difficult to close on a deal. "Many properties we looked at were bank owned, and banks weren't considering us since we were new to the beer business. They looked at us as very high risk. I think I made an offer on seven or eight different buildings before someone took us seriously," Brandon said. "They would much rather have a Subway go into their space rather than taking a risk on a newbie."

The Richters finally found a spot located in a strip mall in Peoria. They signed the deal and began to plan for the build out of the brewery.

With a spot secured, the Richters needed to raise money. Kickstarter worked for other breweries, so the Richters gave it a try. Before they went live, they got word another prospective brewery was planning a similar

Kickstarter campaign, so they held off until the "competing" brewery completed its online funding.

The plan backfired. With a goal of raising $30,000, the Richters topped out at $27,000. Because they didn't attain their goal, they didn't receive a penny. It turned out that two breweries seeking backers over a short period of time in a similar locale were one too many. It was time to regroup.

After being rejected by several banks, they found a small Tucson company that did microloan lending. This lender loved the Richters' story and took a chance on them. Unbeknownst to the Richters at the time, the program was affiliated with the Sam Adams's Brewing the American Dream program, which funded and advised small businesses. Not only did they have access to much needed funding, they also had an invaluable resource of one of America's most successful craft brewers.

Operating under the working name of Mischief Brewing Company, the Richters discovered another startup brewery beat them to the punch and trademarked the name.

Around this time, Brandon found an old picture of his great-grandfather and another man. On the back of the picture was written "Richter and McCarty Brewing Company." It turned out his great-grandfather Moritz Richter was once a brewery owner. The German immigrant landed in Ogden City, Utah, where he and his friend opened a brewery with the help of a minority owner, the legendary Brigham Young. Inspired to carry on the family tradition, Richter Aleworks was born.

Taking possession of their building in August 2015, the couple faced several obstacles to opening. Taking a full year to satisfy inspectors, Richter Aleworks opened December 2016. One very large obstacle still existed. They did not yet have their brewing license. They collaborated with North Mountain Brewing and fellow Colorado Boy graduate Steve McFate, supplementing the remaining taps with guest beers. The first batch of beer was sold in June 2017. Within six months, Richter Aleworks was finally able to produce its own beer.

Richter Aleworks' most popular beer is Hot Fuzz. The beer was inspired when the local fire and police departments were looking to do a fundraiser and asked the brewery if it would participate. Members of both departments came in on brew day and helped brew a saison-style beer made with fresh apricots. The event was a success, and the beer was a hit. From that point forward, customers clamored for Hot Fuzz. An ode to the original brewery name exists in Criminal Mischief, Richter Aleworks' best-selling IPA.

While the Richters may have faced their fair share of challenges along the way, Peoria now has a hometown brewery to call its own, while Brandon and his family can carry on his great-grandfather's tradition as a brewery owner.

Saddle Mountain Brewing Company

When you have a dedicated couple, one with a background in restaurant entrepreneurship and the other in aviation, things are very likely to *take off* quickly. That sums up life once the doors opened at Saddle Mountain Brewery in Goodyear, Arizona.

Jacob Hansen had always been completely enamored, if not obsessed, with aviation. It started when he was an eight-year-old boy living in Arlington, Arizona, just southwest of Buckeye. That was when Jacob first saw, and instantly fell in love with, the Goodyear blimp. The blimp flew over the house, and Jacob was in awe. Dreaming of boarding the famed airship one day, he wrote letters monthly to the Goodyear Tire Company expressing his desire to ride on the blimp. Much to the family's surprise, Goodyear responded and offered the Hansens a four-hour ride on the blimp. From that moment on, Jacob Hansen became an aviation lifer.

From a young age, Jacob wanted to join the Air Force. His older brother was a Navy Seal, prompting Jacob to envision a similar military career. Sadly, Jacob suffered a devastating injury when he was just thirteen, resulting in the loss of his pinky, ring finger and part of the middle finger on his right hand. The injury destroyed any chance of achieving his Air Force dream. Jacob did, however, stay laser focused on aviation. Taking his first solo flight at age sixteen, he had his pilot's license by age twenty.

Jacob got a job as an apprentice at Pierce Aviation, a crop-dusting company, based in Buckeye, Arizona. Accomplished for his age, he was a homeowner and half-owner of a Piper Cub Taildragger airplane in his early twenties. At this point, owning a brewery was nowhere on his radar.

Like Jacob, Laura Hollenstein lived in the shadow of the famed Saddle Mountain, about twelve miles away in neighboring Tonopah, Arizona. Both attended Buckeye High School but did not know each other, Laura being three years Jacob's senior. Like Jacob's mother, Laura was a schoolteacher, teaching at the school she attended from kindergarten through eighth grade. When they met, Laura was drawn to Jacob's work ethic and his dedication.

Shortly after the two began to date, Jacob asked Laura to take a ride in his plane. As the plane rose skyward, the two flew over Saddle Mountain, which separates the towns where each grew up. About one year later, the couple married.

Not knowing what to get Jacob for one particular birthday, Laura purchased a Mr. Beer kit so Jacob could make his own beer at home. A new passion was about to take shape.

Beer brewing supplies and equipment became the norm at gift-giving time, and eventually, Jacob began to brew his own beer recipes. One Christmas, everyone in the family got together and bought Jacob a kegerator so he could serve his beers on draft.

Laura's parents were serial entrepreneurs, creating or refurbishing businesses. These included owning a general store, an RV park, a used car dealership, a beauty salon and a bar and grill. When Laura and her dad, Ray, opened Tin Top Bar & Grill, Laura quit teaching so she could focus on developing the business. Though he was working for Glendale Aviation at the time, Jacob got to experience the operation of a food and beverage establishment.

After the tragedy of 9/11, Jacob's aviation career as a flight instructor stalled. While the overall economy slowed down, no industry was hit harder than the airline industry. Many people stopped flying, and fewer flights were scheduled, meaning fewer pilots were needed. Before long, airlines had a surplus of pilots and weren't looking to hire new ones. Without a steady stream of pilots to train, there was no business for a flight instructor. Jacob eventually got a job at Ameriflight, flying freight and cargo, and later began working for the FAA as a safety inspector.

Wanting to plan for the future, Laura exited the businesses she and her family were involved in so she and Jacob could make their next move. The couple began considering various options, including possibly opening a brewery. Jacob suggested using some of the money, about $8,000, to buy a home brewery system. Not wanting to go down the bar/restaurant path again, Laura was initially against it, especially with a three-year-old child to consider. But Jacob was working an FAA job he didn't particularly enjoy and wanted a change.

While Laura considered the brewery no more than a passing thought, the idea wouldn't leave Jacob's mind. He even started looking at buildings, envisioning what could one day be possible.

"We'd jokingly come up with names for our fictitious brewery," said Laura. "A while later, I received a letter in the mail realizing Jacob had filed paperwork to register the corporate name of his new brewing company, to be known as Saddle Mountain Brewing Company. This took place in 2011."

Realizing Jacob was focused on a dream of becoming a brewery owner, Laura converted part of their garage into a brewery. Once Jacob convinced Laura to look at some buildings, the couple drove all around the west side of Phoenix, looking at potential sites. Eventually they came across the place in Goodyear that would eventually house Saddle Mountain Brewing Company. Wanting to own their place and not exist at the mercy of an unwieldy landlord, the Goodyear location appealed to the couple's business sense because it was for sale.

Jacob and Laura called the City of Goodyear to gauge the city's thoughts about a potential brewery. The city's rules turned out to be archaic. The way the law was written at the time, a person could have a brewery if it didn't take up more than 25 percent of the total space of the building and the beer could only be sold within the confines of that building. Jacob went to Goodyear's planning and zoning department, where he met City Planner Steve Careccia. Jacob asked Steve if the city would consider modifying the antiquated laws.

Steve and Jacob sat down and rewrote the zoning laws pertaining to breweries, hoping to prepare a good case to take to town council and the

Laura and Jacob Hansen, founders of Saddle Mountain Brewing. *Courtesy of Saddle Mountain.*

Goodyear mayor. One rule Goodyear had at the time was that no alcohol could be sold or live music performed within 500 feet of churches, schools and residential areas. The proposed location the Hansens wanted was just 378 feet from a residential area. Steve sat down with a copy of the current law, scratched out "500" and made it "300" feet. Now he had to convince the mayor and town council to go along with his proposed rule changes.

Unless the law was changed, banks wouldn't lend money. The entire process, from start to finish, took nine grueling months. Steve took the proposed law changes to his legislators, and the changes were eventually approved. The brewery could now move forward, sell its beer and have live music performances.

With the laws changed and loan approved, the Hansens became proud owners of a new building. They decided that to succeed on the west side, having a full-service brewpub was their best option. The Hansens believed that the food would be the initial draw but once people tried the beer, they would keep coming back.

While the "corporate" name of the company was Saddle Mountain Brewing Company, the couple continued to think about different operating names and themes. While the name Saddle Mountain evoked thoughts of the cowboys and horses, Jacob wanted to pay homage to his love of aviation. He weaved aviation themes throughout the majority of his beers, and they decorated their new facility accordingly.

One of Jacob's beers was called Taildragger. The couple loved the name and strongly considered it as the brewery name. However, having already filed all the paperwork under the name Saddle Mountain Brewing Company, the couple decided to keep that as the brewpub (and corporate entity) name, while "Taildragger" became the name for the line of beers.

Saddle Mountain Brewing Company officially opened to the public on October 24, 2014. Opening a brewpub with a full menu was exactly the right call for this burgeoning area of Goodyear, Arizona. Saddle Mountain was well received from day one. "Defining good beer for generations" is the mantra the company lives by, and the Hansens have clearly achieved success in this realm, evident by the diverse clientele generally found at the brewpub.

Located about a mile from the spring training home of the Cleveland Indians and Cincinnati Reds, Saddle Mountain is an oasis for tourists and fans during the popular months of February and March. That doesn't deter the locals who patronize the brewpub year-round, anxiously awaiting head brewer Neal Huttenhow's latest creations.

While not the brewery's first head brewer, Huttenhow came on board several months into Saddle Mountain's existence. Having brewed previously at the popular breweries Four Peaks and Rock Bottom, Huttenhow was the missing piece that completed a solid team with the Hansens.

Five of the regular beers that appeared on Saddle Mountain's lineup were Jacob's original homebrew recipes, including a popular imperial red ale known as "300 Foot Steve." This beer was named in honor of Goodyear city planner Steve Careccia, who helped get the laws rewritten so the brewery could legally exist, a fitting tribute to a man who helped make the whole thing possible.

Another popular brew called Hop Snob is a tribute to a family friend and hoppy beer lover, Deanne Forney. Ray's Gold, made with Nugget hops, is named after Laura's dad, Ray Hollenstein, who was an amateur gold hunter always seeking his gold nuggets.

Warhawk Cream Ale is the brewery's top seller due to its light-drinking nature and lower alcohol content. Chasing Tail Amber Ale is also extremely popular. The light-bodied Belgian Wit known as 5G is a fan favorite, perfect in the hot Phoenix climate.

Outside of Jacob's five "house" recipes, the remainder of the beer lineup is the brainchild of award-winning head brewer Neal Huttenhow, who regularly has seasonal and specialty offerings available.

Saddle Mountain Brewing made an immediate connection as a neighborhood destination place. The brewery was voted fifth-most popular place where locals spend money, the four companies finishing above them all being chains. Some of their beers also fared well in local competitions, winning medals at the Arizona Strong Beer Festival in 2016 with a gold for 300 Foot Steve and in 2017 with a bronze for Three's Company, a Belgian Trippel. Clan-Destine Scotch Ale took the best-in-show award at the 2018 Made in the Shade Festival in Flagstaff.

Success was not limited to the neighborhood, however. Saddle Mountain made the world take notice after Clan-Destine, a malt-forward, caramel-like Scottish ale, won the silver medal at the World Beer Cup in 2018 after claiming the gold medal at the Great American Beer Festival 2017. The world began to discover what the locals of Goodyear, Arizona, already knew: Saddle Mountain Brewing Company was for real.

The love affair between brewery and community is definitely a two-way street. Participating in local charities is an important part of the Saddle Mountain fabric. One of the charities the brewery supports is the Fighter Country Partnership, affiliated with Luke Air Force Base on Phoenix's far

Jacob Hansen living his other passion, aviation. *Courtesy of Saddle Mountain.*

west side. Because of the participation with the charity, Jacob was nominated to be an honorary commander at Luke AFB, which he anxiously accepted. One of the perks of this huge honor was getting to fly in an F-16, a lifelong dream of Jacob's, bringing the story full circle.

The unfortunate childhood injury that cost Jacob the opportunity to see his Air Force dream come to fruition would stop him no longer. During his time working as a flight instructor at Glendale Aviation, Jacob instructed a flight student named Ray Naylor. Naylor eventually earned his commercial license and went on to become an F-16 fighter pilot in the Air Force. Naylor later moved into the neighborhood in which the Hansens lived, and the two became friends.

After accepting the honorary commander nomination at Luke AFB, Jacob finally got to have his commemorative flight in the F-16. In what seemed like a Hollywood movie script, his pilot for that flight was the very man he trained years earlier, his former student turned friend, Ray Naylor.

Jacob Hansen was able to fulfil not one, but two life dreams in a way he never could have imagined. The dreams were made possible by the existence and community connection that developed because of Saddle Mountain Brewing Company, the crown jewel brewery of the western suburbs of Phoenix.

Jacob now has his own business as a designated pilot examiner called Flightworks LLC, continuing the aviation theme in his life, while Laura, with her years of experience running her former bar and grill, now runs the day-to-day activities at Saddle Mountain. The couple's unique individual talents make the operation a smooth-running machine.

According to Jacob, "Laura was the designer of the final look of the brewery/restaurant and is the heart and soul of the continuing operations of the brewery and restaurant. She works the daily toils of management and oversight, along with marketing and creativity that makes the place the great brewery it is. She is truly the reason for the continued success of the business."

A FINAL TOAST

Professional brewing in Phoenix dates back almost two hundred years. The names change and the people come and go, but one thing remains the same: Phoenicians love their beer. Today, they have more options for locally brewed beer than ever before. New breweries seemingly pop up every few weeks, expanding the offerings to satisfy even the pickiest of palates.

This book sets out to provide a history of brewing in Phoenix, from its inception to the modern-day brewery explosion. While an attempt was made to include as many breweries as possible, by no means did, or could, this book tell *every* brewery's story. Many breweries not covered within these pages have devout fans and brew fine beers, breweries such as State 48, Dubina, 12 West, Desert Eagle, the Perch, Blasted Barley, Loco Patron and Mesquite River, among others.

The future is bright for beer lovers in and around Phoenix, with no reason to believe that will change anytime soon. Just as the Phoenix once rose from the ashes, the Phoenix brewing scene continues to do the same.

ABOUT THE AUTHOR

Former professional brewer, Certified Cicerone and one of two Master-level BJCP beer judges in the state of Arizona, Dave Clark is an established beer and music journalist. A Phoenix resident since 2014, Dave contributes regularly to publications such as *Brew Your Own*, *Zymurgy*, *Beer Connoisseur* and *Beer Advocate*. The former beer scribe for *New Times* and *Entertainer Magazine*, Clark is a past president of S.N.O.B. homebrew club. He enjoys performing locally as a singer/guitarist, supporting his album *Rock City*, and, naturally, visiting local breweries and watering holes. www.brewsician.com.

Visit us at
www.historypress.com